Endorsements for
A Grace Revealed

It isn't difficult to find a writer who tells us what to believe or how to behave. Jerry Sittser has something far better in mind: that who we are in the circumstances of our lives is a *story*, that Jesus and redemption are actually *livable*, and that right now we are in the middle of something *lived*, a *story*. This is rare.

> —EUGENE H. PETERSON, Professor of Emeritus of Spiritual Theology, Regent College, Vancouver, B.C.

Jerry Sittser is a man marked by the grace of God. When he speaks, teaches, and writes, we need to listen. *A Grace Revealed* is filled with insightful encouragement for those on the rugged journey through life. I read all of Jerry's books—he's one of my favorite authors.

> —DR. DENNIS RAINEY, President, FamilyLife

Out of a life both broken and blessed, Jerry Sittser tells the story of redemption—both his and ours. *A Grace Revealed* offers a clear theological line of sight to Christ's redeeming rescue of our past, present, and future. It is a warmly annotated guide to lavish grace for the most slumping of souls. The book seized me with hope.

—BILL ROBINSON, President Emeritus,
Whitworth University, Spokane, Washington

Jerry Sittser has written a remarkable book. *A Grace Revealed* is a book of three narratives. One story is his own, which he brings to the middle point. Another story is our own, which he encourages us to trace into our middle point. The third story, which he calls "The Story," points to the one who is the Redeemer of every story, Jesus of Nazareth. Sittser is sensitive, realistic, wise, and very helpful in the ways he journeys with his readers throughout the three stories. His own faith in Christ becomes a very encouraging pastoral presence throughout. I warmly endorse this book.

—EARL F. PALMER

A SEQUEL TO *A GRACE DISGUISED*

A GRACE REVEALED

HOW GOD REDEEMS *the* STORY

OF YOUR LIFE

JERRY SITTSER

ZONDERVAN

ZONDERVAN.com/
AUTHOR**TRACKER**
follow your favorite authors

We want to hear from you. Please send your comments about this book to us in care of zreview@zondervan.com. Thank you.

ZONDERVAN

A Grace Revealed
Copyright © 2012 by Gerald L. Sittser

This title is also available as a Zondervan ebook. Visit www.zondervan.com/ebooks.

This title is also available in a Zondervan audio edition. Visit www.zondervan.fm.

Requests for information should be addressed to:

Zondervan, *Grand Rapids, Michigan 49530*

Library of Congress Cataloging-in-Publication Data

Sittser, Gerald Lawson, 1950 –
     A grace revealed : how God redeems the story of your life / Gerald L. Sittser.
          p. cm.
     ISBN 978-0-310-24325-0 (hardcover)
     1. Christian life. 2. Redemption — Christianity. I. Title.
BV4509.5.S575   2012
248.4 — dc23   2012016763

All Scripture quotations, unless otherwise indicated, are taken from The Holy Bible, *New International Version®, NIV®.* Copyright © 1973, 1978, 1984, 2011 by Biblica, Inc.™ Used by permission. All rights reserved worldwide.

Any Internet addresses (websites, blogs, etc.) and telephone numbers in this book are offered as a resource. They are not intended in any way to be or imply an endorsement by Zondervan, nor does Zondervan vouch for the content of these sites and numbers for the life of this book.

Published in association with the literary agency of Ann Spangler and Company, 1420 Pontiac Road S.E., Grand Rapids, MI 49506.

Cover design: Studio Gearbox
Cover and interior photography: Veer®
Interior design: Beth Shagene

Printed in the United States of America

---

12 13 14 15 16 17 /DCI/ 21 20 19 18 17 16 15 14 13 12 11 10 9 8 7 6 5 4 3 2 1

To Patricia,
who is a gift of grace, goodness,
and beauty to so many.

Contents

Acknowledgments

An author writes a book, but a community participates in the process. I am the grateful beneficiary of a wonderful community of friends who contributed, both directly and indirectly, to the birthing of this book. Words simply fail to express my debt to them and my love for them.

I want to begin by mentioning the dear friends who surrounded me early on in our story, long before I ever thought of writing a book about grace, whether disguised or revealed. Julie Pyle offered to care for John while he was still very young and very injured, even though she had just given birth to her third child, and Monica and Andrea served our family as successive — and successful — nannies. What would we have done without these good and godly women, still so dear to our family? My sister, Diane, and brother-in-law, Jack, such good friends, counseled and encouraged me as I figured out how to do life as a widowed father of three.

My children, Catherine, David, and John, are gifts of God to me. Now grown and gone, they have become my friends in addition to being my children. I cannot speak for how other fathers feel about their children, but in my mind few have been as blessed as I am. I am so proud of them. I am even more blessed now by having Morgan and Taylor, my two stepdaughters, as well as Jacob, Kelli, and Annalise, my children-in-law, as members of the family. Nor should I forget to mention my first grandchild, Gideon. It is almost too much to comprehend.

A number of people read this book and suggested revisions. Five colleagues and friends at Whitworth — Jim Edwards, Adam Neder, Kent McDonald, Kamesh Sankaran, and Jonathan Moo — offered excellent criticism, always in a spirit of love. Katie Wisenor, Krisi Sonneland, Kae Johnson, Charissa Strope, Craig and Maxine Lammers, Avrilia and Dan Autrey, Andrea Palpant Dilley, Howard Wilcock, Mark Muilenburg, and Chris Stolcis read an early draft and provided helpful comments that shaped later drafts. Chris in particular read it from a perspective few others have.

My editor at Zondervan, Sandy Vander Zicht, kept urging me to weave theology and story together, something I was hesitant to do. She persisted in holding me to high standards and, once she started the editing process, made suggestions that improved the manuscript on almost every page. My former editor, Ann Spangler, helped to shape the project, too, and cheered me on once I began the process of writing. Verlyn Verbrugge applied his watchful eye to the final editing process; he has turned attention to detail into a virtual art form. The team at Zondervan committed themselves to getting this book out as best they could as a sequel and companion to *A Grace Disguised*, my first book with Zondervan. They demonstrated professional competence and provided solid support all along the way. Finally, the Service Station, my favorite local coffee shop, became my home-away-from-home as I worked on an early draft. The folks who work there are great people.

One person in particular stood at my side from beginning to end, listening to my ideas, asking good questions, reading drafts, urging me to do my best, and praying over this project. Patricia invested in this book like no one else. Every day she shows me what a spouse, partner, and friend can and should be. I dedicate this book to her in a spirit of gratitude and joy. Who could have ever predicted our stories would converge as they have? Only God has that kind of imagination, humor, and goodness.

Preface

O n the eve of the weddings of my three children I gave each of them a photo album as a wedding gift. At first glance it would seem that the albums consisted of little more than a random collection of photos, each photo capturing a fleeting moment in their lives. But as you can probably guess, the albums, containing perhaps a hundred photos, tell the story of how the children grew and changed between birth and marriage. A narrative thread runs through each one.

Story is the theme of this book. God has written and played the key role in the story of salvation, which promises to redeem our stories — mending what is broken, healing what is sick, making right what has gone so wrong. This glorious story of redemption turns on the work of Jesus Christ, the Son of God and Savior of the world, who came into this world to make us new, which he accomplished through his life, death, and resurrection. It is all his doing, a gift of pure grace. But we must receive this gift and make it our own, like children growing into adults. Redemption means becoming the new persons we already are in Jesus Christ. In fact, we can *become* new in Christ because we already *are* new in Christ.

If you have glanced at the Table of Contents, you have already noticed that I take the theme of story quite literally. The chapter titles make that clear enough: "Characters in Search of a Story," "A Story in Search of Characters," "Scene and Setting," "Plot," and "Author." I realized early on that I could not write a book about story if I were not true to its very nature, for all stories include characters, scene and setting, plot, author, and the like. This is true of the biblical story; it is equally true of yours and mine. The organization of the book, therefore, reflects this theme.

I also realized that I could hardly write a book about the redemptive story if I did not tell stories along the way. Here I faced a choice. Books of this kind tend to string together a series of disconnected anecdotes and quotes that illustrate the various theological points made along the way. The theology unites the book, not the stories. But I wondered if that was the right literary strategy to follow in a book about story, for it would seem to undermine the very point I was trying to make. I decided, therefore, to use one story as an illustration of *the* story, in order to show how our human stories fit into the redemptive story. Once I made this decision, I thought it best to use the one story with which I am most familiar, namely, my own.

You will notice along the way, therefore, that I reflect on my story — really, my family's story — as it was unfolding during the writing of the book. On several occasions I refer to my daughter Catherine as being pregnant; she has since given birth. My first grandchild, Gideon, was born just a few weeks ago. Continual change is the nature of story itself, which I try to capture in the book.

Still, this book is not a memoir. It tells my family story, but only to explain and explore the theme of redemption. I invite you to read this book with *your* story in mind, not mine. The story of redemption is like no other, for it promises to envelop and transform all other stories, however sensational or mundane, tragic or happy. I see myself as a witness to this truth: God redeems our stories through his. If you dare to surrender yourself to God, he will take up the story of your life and integrate it into the great story of salvation, turning it into something so extraordinary that you will be tempted to think that it was all a beautiful dream.

CHAPTER 1

Weathered and Beautiful

In 2006, my kids and I took a family vacation to Banff National Park, located in the Canadian Rockies. We hiked some forty miles in five days, exploring many of the great features of this magnificent park. Along the way, we kept noticing a certain kind of pine tree, the white bark pine, dotting the landscape, especially at higher elevations. Clinging to rocky cliffs overlooking pristine lakes, massive glaciers, and deep valleys, they looked like sentinels keeping watch over the world. Each one was obviously weathered—trunks gnarled; limbs broken off; bark roughed up by wind, rain, sleet, and snow; clumps of needles stealing bits of sunlight; clawlike roots gripping rocky slopes. These trees had passed the test of time and survived, sculpted by the elements into extraordinary works of art. They were truly beautiful—not beautiful like a child's innocent and delicate face, but beautiful like the carved and aged face of a lifelong fisherman or farmer. These trees were strong and seasoned, full of years and memory and character.

Extraordinary Beauty

Those trees symbolize what I believe God wants to accomplish in our lives, which is to work complete redemption.

He wants to use the harsh conditions of life to shape us—and eventually the whole world—into something extraordinarily beautiful. Redemption promises to transform us, completely so. Once broken, we become whole again; once selfish and insecure, we become stately and serene and self-giving; once rabid sinners, we become glorious saints. In short, God purposes to claim us as his own—no matter how far we are from him, how fallen into sin, how lost and lonely. He wants to restore us to a right relationship with him and to remake us according to the image of Jesus Christ, which will ultimately lead to the renewal of the whole world. This is God's doing, from beginning to end. <u>God is the one</u>—the only one—who can, does, and will work redemption.

Redemption has become significant to me, and for very personal reasons, as I will soon explain. It is a biblical term, too. But like other biblical terms, such as *justification, reconciliation,* and *atonement*, it seems alien and even intimidating to us, the religious equivalent of an algebraic equation. We don't use the term much in regular speech, and we don't usually ask people, "How's your redemption going?" which would make us appear insufferably religious and weird. The word might occupy a place in our religious vocabulary, useful to toss around at church or in a Bible study, but it hardly seems relevant to daily life.

I want to reclaim the word and make it understandable, useful, and meaningful for ordinary life. It is a rich term, and it captures the entire scope and drama of the biblical story, which is redemptive at its core. I hope to define and explain the term in such a familiar and practical way that it will make a genuine difference in your life. This is the goal set before me.

But I need something from you, too, which I am going to ask for up front. I want you to read this book with your own life in mind, your ordinary life, the real life you are currently living, whether you are young or old; single, married, divorced, or widowed; employed, unemployed, or retired; rooted in a community or profoundly lonely; satisfied with your circumstances or disappointed with them; elated about life or discontented, restless, even depressed. Redemption is the work of Jesus Christ applied to the unfolding story of life, your life and my life. It turns gospel truth into a dramatic narrative and makes theology applicable to everyday life. Redemption happens through God's involvement in the ordinary circumstances of life, no matter what those circumstances happen to be. You are not beyond God's redemptive reach—not now, not ever. So I ask you to read this book in light of your life as it is right now.

THE STORY BEHIND THE STORY

I should probably explain how I came to write both *A Grace Disguised*, which was published in 1996, and now this sequel, *A Grace Revealed*. Many years ago my family suffered a terrible tragedy. My mother, Grace, who was visiting us for the weekend, my wife, Lynda, and my youngest daughter, Diana Jane, were all killed in a drunken-driving accident. I survived the accident, as did my other three children, then very young. That the accident occurred over twenty years ago means that I have gained a great deal of perspective over time. I am no longer looking ahead into some terrible void, as I was right after the accident occurred, seeing nothing but darkness. I am now looking back, some twenty years later, on what has happened since. Not that life has been easy. This book will not tell a sweet and simple story about tragedy leading to triumph. Still, I hope it will tell a redemptive story.

In the months and years following the accident, I realized that the tragedy itself, however catastrophic, could actually play a less significant role than what God could do with it and how I would respond to it. Would it cause a downward spiral of destruction, or would it illumine and illustrate a story of grace and redemption? I chose to believe it would tell a redemptive story, trusting that God was still God, sovereign and wise and good, however miserable I felt and distant God seemed to be. I set my mind to ponder the redemptive course that was laid out before me, shrouded, as it was, in mystery.

What, I began to ask, does redemption really mean, given my unwanted and undesirable circumstances? Where does it lead? How does God work redemption in our lives? These questions—and many others as well—brooded inside me. How could a grace disguised in an accident become a grace revealed, discovered, and experienced in the unfolding story of my life? Shattered as I was, I purposed to learn as much as I could and catch glimpses of how God works to redeem human life, including my own.

But this is a book for you, not for me. My story will make its way into the narrative from time to time. Still, I am more interested in helping you discern how God is working redemption in *your* life. This is why I invite you to read this book in light of your own circumstances. An accident and its aftermath provided the setting for my story, like props on a stage. What is the setting for your story? How can you play your role in that story well, even if it is a role you would never have chosen? How can you exercise the kind of faith that will give God room and freedom to do his work?

If anything, I share my own story with a certain degree of ambivalence. My editor and I even disagreed over how much of my story to include in the manuscript, I wanting less, she urging more. As I have already mentioned, some fifteen years ago I wrote a book about loss, written in the wake of the tragedy that so dramatically changed the life of my family. The first draft of *A Grace Disguised: How the Soul Grows through Loss* was entirely theological, telling readers what to *think* about loss. My friends liked the draft well enough but commented that it was too abstract and impersonal. "You have to tell your story," they said to me. "If you don't, readers won't be able to identify with it, or with you." After much prayer and reflection, I chose to tell the family story, though I felt acutely self-conscious about it.

I faced two problems. First, I didn't want our family to be defined by the tragedy, as if we were little more than "the family that lost three generations of women in one accident." This concern—an entirely legitimate one, it seems to me—

caused me to focus attention on our response to the tragedy rather than the tragedy itself, on God's gracious intervention after the accident rather than his apparent absence during the accident.

It was also important to me that our story not overshadow anyone else's, which would be easy to do considering how dramatic it was. I believed then, as I do now, that our loss was no more difficult than the losses many others have experienced, nor was our pain any more acute. I have received thousands of letters since *A Grace Disguised* was published, and each one reminded me that people experience catastrophic loss in a variety of ways, all of them bad. Mine was no more severe than others. For example, I never had to face rejection; I never had to care for a loved one with permanent disabilities; I never had to absorb one loss after another, the first setting off a chain reaction, with many more to follow. Taken as a whole, my story has been quite good. My children and I simply had to adjust to a severe trauma that swept over us like a tidal wave.

In a matter of a few years, our life as a family of four returned to a normal routine. How much can I really say about it? Like most people, I worked a job (a convenient, meaningful, and flexible job at that!), reared three children, and managed a home. I learned to make life work. All things considered, our lives have been quite normal. Now grown, my kids are thriving. There is only so much I can write about such an ordinary life, except to recount how normal it was. Maybe this is the point. God works redemption, whether life takes a dramatic turn or continues on its usual course. In the end, redemption is about God—who he is and how he works. He is the author, we the characters.

Still, I believe that telling stories is necessary and important, for it is impossible to understand redemption apart from story—the biblical story, of course, but also my story and your story. This is why I have chosen to include stories in this book (mostly mine, because it is the story I know best), for they help to explain what redemption means in concrete terms and how it applies to life as we live it from day to day.

The Paradox

Redemption is rooted in a paradox, which can be summed up in a simple phrase: we become who we already are in Jesus Christ. Jesus Christ *is* redemption; Jesus Christ is also the one who *works* redemption. We are already redeemed through his work on the cross and in the resurrection, and we are in the process of being redeemed by the Holy Spirit's ongoing work in our lives. Both are true—the being and the becoming, the position and the process, the already and the not yet. It is this paradox—lived out over time and in ordinary life—I want to explore.

I carry a vivid memory of the birth of each of my children. I remember the birth doctor laying our babies on the chest of Lynda, who gazed at them with such fierce and tender eyes. These were children who grew inside her, who were known and loved before they ever took a breath. There they were, lying so innocently and peacefully on her chest. Little did we know then what would happen in the years to come. Little did we realize how glorious and harsh life would be, how strange and mysterious and wonderful. We knew nothing of friendships they would have, of sports they would play, of music they would make, of vacations they would take. We knew nothing of neighborhood and family friends, of nannies and newcomers to the family. And we knew nothing of an accident that would send us reeling in an entirely new direction.

As I recall the joys and sorrows I did not know, nor could have anticipated, at the birth of my children, my mind wanders back to Banff National Park. I have two photos in an album, situated side by side. One is dated August 1991. Four little children stand at the shore of Lake Louise in Banff National Park, the calm azure water stretching out behind them, a massive glacier looming in the background. The other is dated July 2006. Only three children stand at the shore of Lake Louise; they are tall and strong and beautiful, and they are making a silly pose, smiling playfully and contagiously. The same lake stretches out behind them; the same glacier looms in the background.

Quite by accident, they are standing in the same place they were when that first photo was taken in 1991. But a sibling is absent, and so is a mother. I stare at those photos from time to time, my mind reviewing all that happened between those two occasions—so much that was hard, so much that was lovely and holy. The time between those two photos constitutes a long chapter in our story, a story of paradox. A family, already redeemed through Jesus Christ, experiences redemption as an ongoing story of suffering, grace, and growth.

WHERE WE ARE HEADED

So redemption involves the story of how God reclaims and restores us into a living relationship with himself so that we can become the people God has always intended us to be. Redemption is entirely God's doing, which makes the Christian faith the exact opposite of a self-help religion. God works redemption through his Son, Jesus Christ; it is through Jesus Christ that all of life is made well and whole, all of life is healed and restored, all of life is put right. Jesus makes redemption a living reality, even if we don't experience it in exactly the way we had hoped, wanted, and expected. He is the one who turns a young sapling into a weathered and beautiful tree.

In the course of this book I want to explore four essential truths about redemption.

Redemption involves a story. Time is the medium in which it unfolds, which is why the Bible has essentially a narrative structure. The biblical story provides clues for how we can understand our own redemptive story, as if following a kind of map of the spiritual terrain in which God works.

God is the author of the redemptive story, from beginning to end. As sovereign Lord of the universe he is writing the story

—it is thus *his* story; we are only playing a role in it. Still, as characters in the story, we do have freedom to make choices and thus to shape the plot, though that freedom is only true freedom when, in the course of the story, we surrender it to God and do his will.

2. *The setting and circumstances in which we live—however desirable or miserable—always play a limited role and, if submitted to God, can actually play a useful role.* There are no better or worse redemptive circumstances that would somehow give one a spiritual advantage, making it easier for some more than others to be redeemed. If anything, what we perceive as favorable circumstances might actually put us at a spiritual disadvantage, lulling us into a dangerous complacency.

3. *The goal of redemption is not immediate happiness as we might define it now, but holiness of life; not the good life as we imagine it on Earth, but the perfection of Heaven itself.* In this case, Heaven is not some "place" out or up there, perhaps on the other side of Jupiter. It is rather a completion, enlargement, and perfection of what we experience in this life. Thus, everything that happens in this life spills over into that other and greater life, pointing beyond itself to reality as God knows, sees, and experiences it.

LOOKING BACK AFTER TWENTY YEARS

I still sometimes reflect on the accident and its aftermath, placing myself once again in those terrible circumstances. When I turned my gaze forward and peered into the future some twenty years ago, I could see nothing but darkness and feel nothing but anguish. I believed there was grace available to me, but it was grace disguised by the sorrow, pain, and mystery of tragedy and suffering. When I look back now and reflect on the last twenty years, I see grace revealed, discovered, and experienced, made abundantly evident by the forces that have shaped my—really, our—story. It is a story of a sapling being gradually formed into a weathered and beautiful tree. It is still going on, too. Our story will continue to unfold until God is finished and his works of art are complete.

CHAPTER 2

Characters in Search
of a Story

I grew up in a liberal mainline Protestant church that did little to explain the gospel and model authentic faith to me or to my friends, most of whom rejected the faith. At least that is the way I saw it then, though time and maturity have softened my harsh judgment. During my teen years I, too, rebelled against God and the church, being confused about both. I neglected to use my abilities, such as they were, spurned moral standards, and chose instead to indulge my appetites. My high school academic record provides ample evidence of my lostness, foolishness, and immaturity. I eventually grew weary of the triviality of sin and the superficiality of my life, though I had no idea what to do about it.

Following my sophomore year in college, I landed a summer job as a camp counselor. My spiritual awakening began during staff training when I fell into a long conversation with a local pastor who was visiting the camp. After quickly realizing I had no idea what true Christianity was, he explained the Christian faith in a way I could understand. He was all too clear and winsome. At the end of the conversation I said, in a tone of conceit and defiance, "If that is what it means to be Christian, I never want to be one."

Still, his words became a torment, piercing and probing

me at every turn. I wrestled and resisted the gospel for perhaps a month before admitting I was in desperate need of God. I fought the good fight of unbelief and finally yielded to grace. Standing alone one night on the shores of Lake Michigan, I literally bowed my knee, repented of my sins as best I could, asked God to forgive me, and surrendered my life to him. *repent, ask, surrender*

Such a story is not unusual, at least not since the eighteenth century, when conversion emerged as the requisite first step in becoming a Christian. Literally hundreds of millions of people around the world have experienced a conversion similar to mine. Nevertheless, I discovered over time that, sincere as I was, my conversion was incomplete. How I gave my life to God is important, of course; but equally important is how I would grow up in God. What good is an experience if it remains little more than an insular event disconnected from a larger narrative? It's like a wedding that never leads to the actual experience of marriage.

I discovered the importance of that connection — between my conversion story and a larger story — when I studied the American Puritan movement some years later. Puritans have a less-than-stellar reputation, but they were far more insightful and influential than you might think. For one, they understood conversion as a process. Before churchgoers could take communion for the first time and thus become church members, they had to tell their conversion story to church leaders. And a *story* was exactly what leaders wanted to hear, too. They were not looking for perfection; they only wanted to see signs of authenticity and find evidence of a faith that had taken root and begun to grow, a sapling on its way to becoming a weathered tree. Had the candidates for membership passed through periods of doubt, but then resolved the doubt and settled into a stable faith? Were they struggling to overcome a sinful habit? Did they make promises to God, only to break them, but then, returning to God, repent of their sins? Could they tell a story of God's faithfulness in suffering? It was the narrative of conversion — not simply the moment of conversion — that mattered.

As it is, no conversion occurs in a vacuum, disconnected from some larger story. This was certainly true for me. I had a past that led up to my conversion and a future that flowed out of it. My experience fit into a grand narrative that is still unfolding. For example, the context of my story at the time of my conversion was also significant. My parents were on the brink of a divorce, precipitated by my dad's infidelities, and my dad was facing financial problems that ultimately ended in bankruptcy and a brief stint in jail. I had personal problems as well; I was insecure and sarcastic, given to excess, confused about life.

Conversion promised to help me escape those problems, or so I thought at the time. In returning "home," as the Prodigal Son did, I turned away from my sinful past and its problems. I soon discovered, however, that my problems followed me home and resisted leaving. Conversion marked only the beginning of my story. I was new in Christ, but I still had to *become* new. I was a Christian, to be sure; but I still had to figure out what being Christian meant, what it promised and required, and how it would change my life. I was like an actor who had landed a role in a play; but I had only a vague idea of what the role was and what the play was about. I was a character in search of a story, as all of us are, longing to discover how our lives fit into some larger narrative that has meaning and purpose.

meaning

NEW CREATION

My father's death in the year 2000 reinforced my understanding of how conversion fits into a bigger story. He lived a hard life and made many bad decisions, though toward the end of his life he turned to God. My sister and I were at his bedside during his last days. Just a few days before he died he asked me to do his memorial service, saying I was the only one who really understood the whole story. I chose for my text 2 Corinthians 5:16–17: "So from now on," Paul writes, "we regard no one from a worldly point of view. Though we once regarded Christ in this way, we do so no longer. Therefore, if anyone is in Christ, the new creation has come: The old has gone, the new is here!" It is an audacious text, and it was audacious of me to use it at my dad's memorial service. He was far from behaving like a "new creation"; if viewed from a human point of view, he fell far short.

But don't we all, really? The entire passage pivots on Paul's view of Jesus Christ. At one time, Paul confesses, he

not perfection

viewed Jesus from "a worldly point of view"—as an imposter, fraud, troublemaker, and traitor to the Jewish religion —which made Paul want to rid the world of the nuisance and threat that Jesus was. He viewed most other people— especially Gentiles—in a similarly negative light. Everything changed, however, after he came to know Jesus as he really is, the Son of God and Savior of the world. Consequently, he changed his mind about everyone else, too. Through Christ people can become new creations, regardless of background, ethnicity, or religious pedigree. Jesus Christ makes all things new. He made Paul new; he made my dad new; he made me new. It is that simple and clear. Christ does it all, completely and perfectly.

The problem is, none of us actually lives that way. We might be new in Christ, but we don't behave in a way that seems new. If anything, there is still a lot of "old" in us. Paul addresses this issue, too. He was passionately devoted to following and serving Jesus. He wanted to know Christ, share in his sufferings, and attain to the resurrection of the dead, and he strived to make progress toward perfection. But like all of us, he fell short and failed.

What kept him going, especially if progress came slowly, or not at all? "Not that I have already obtained all this, or have already arrived at my goal, but I press on to take hold of that for which Christ Jesus took hold of me" (Philippians 3:12). Paul's use of "press on" implies serious engagement and hard work. He purposed to strive after Christ and Christlikeness, having confidence that Christ Jesus "took hold of me." Paul belonged to Jesus. Whatever he achieved amounted to nothing more than becoming who he already was in Christ, a new creation. Thus he could write, "continue to work out your own salvation with fear and trembling," which implies effort and discipline. But then he adds, "for it is God who works in you to will and to act in order to fulfill his good purpose" (Philippians 2:12–13).

Paul knew that God had accomplished everything for him in and through Jesus Christ, which is why he called it grace. He could therefore pursue a life of godliness in freedom, for he was striving for nothing more than what was already his:

> And we know that in all things God works for the good of those who love him, who have been called according to his purpose. For those God foreknew he also predestined to be conformed to the image of his Son, that he might be the firstborn among many brothers and sisters. And those he predestined, he also called; those he called, he also justified; those he justified, he also glorified. (Romans 8:28–30)

This passage is startling because it is clear God does it all, from beginning to end, from justification to glorification, from calling to conforming. Yet Paul did not respond to this truth by becoming passive. It inspired, empowered, and motivated him. He realized that his entire life on earth was a glorious experience of traveling to a destination at which he had already arrived, becoming who he already was. This is equally true for all of us, whether we have succeeded beyond our wildest dreams or, as we will observe in the following story, failed so miserably that we lost all reason to hope for any kind of redemption at all.

SUNDAY'S STORY

As I mentioned in the first chapter, many years ago I wrote a book about suffering, which grew out of years of reflection over the loss of my wife, mother, and daughter. Doing what my friends suggested was my "duty," I wrote *A Grace Disguised* some four years after the accident. However right and good, it was an unpleasant task that brought me no comfort, and it did nothing to explain or justify the accident, which has remained, to this day, a tragic, bewildering, wasteful event.

After writing the book, I surrendered it to God and walked away from it, choosing instead to concentrate on what was immediately at hand, namely, the ordinary duties of being a father and a professor. I assumed that writing the book would be the end of it, like purging a ghost, but that turned out not to be the case. In the years since the book was published, I have received many letters, calls, and emails from readers who, after reading my story, wanted to tell me theirs. A letter from Sunday Pearson especially stands out because it so vividly illustrates the power and the mystery of God's redeeming work. I share Sunday's story with her permission.

In the mid-1980s, a young California police officer named Chuck Stephens was shot in a drug bust. Though he survived the shooting, doctors pronounced him brain-dead on arrival at the hospital. The family decided after days of wrenching discussion, reflection, and prayer, to take him off life support. They then kept vigil until he took his last breath. The young man who died was Sunday's brother. She told me that her brother's death was especially bitter to the family because they had already lost another brother to cancer at age thirteen. The accused murderer, a drug dealer named Fred, was put on trial, convicted, and imprisoned. Sunday did not bother to attend the trial and never knew what happened to him. She was simply too intent on survival in the wake of her brother's murder.

In the years that followed, Sunday did her best to resume an ordinary life. She loved her husband and reared her children and excelled at her work with the Army Corps of Engineers. She settled into a routine and reestablished equilibrium. She rarely thought about Fred. "He was buried deep inside a psychological drawer that remained shut tight. It was easier that way." Still, God was quietly at work, burrowing deeply into her heart and working redemption. "While life was going on around me," she wrote, "God worked on my bruised and broken heart and made me aware of just how much he loves me."

After several years, Sunday began to think about Fred more often, as if those terrible memories were being awakened from slumber. She was surprised when she realized one day that she really had forgiven him, though with little fanfare, emotion, or even awareness. It happened gradually and unnoticeably, like a spring thaw. The passing of years and her growth in faith had extinguished the anger that might have lingered in her heart, thus sparing her from becoming bitter or plotting revenge. Sunday didn't tell anyone about this realization, however, assuming that she — and everyone else — would be happier if she kept the drawer of the past shut tight and locked. But God had something else in mind.

Some twenty-five years after her brother's death, Sunday heard God tell her — quite literally, as she reported to me — that he wanted her to meet Fred. "Isn't it enough that I have forgiven him?" she asked God. To which God replied, "No, it isn't enough." Then God gave her a message for Fred, which she remembers word for word: "Tell Fred that I love him. Tell him that I love him so much that I sent my only Son, Jesus, to die for his sins." That was the first message. But there was a second one, too. "Tell Fred that it is not too late to become the man that I designed him to be."

Although she was disturbed and confused, Sunday immediately went to work to carry out her mission. It took time, patience, and persistence, but she eventually succeeded in locating Fred. People who knew the California prison system warned her, however, that she would not succeed in arranging a meeting with him, the bureaucracy being nearly impossible to navigate. Sunday didn't let that stop her. She wrote to Fred, asking for permission to visit him. He responded almost immediately, saying he had always wondered if the day would come when a member of Chuck's family would contact him. He was both relieved and terrified by the prospect of a meeting. So the day eventually came when two strangers, one a victim, the other a perpetrator, were about to meet face-to-face for the first time.

I imagine the scene in my mind. A man sits in a cell. He receives a letter from a person whose name he doesn't recognize. As he reads it, he is shocked to discover it is the sister of the man he murdered. In disbelief, he reads that she wants to meet him. He puts the letter down and stares at the walls of his cell. He wonders why she wants to see him. Does she want to accuse him? Punish him? Tell him how miserable her life has been? Spit poison into his face?

I imagine a second scene. A woman sits at the breakfast table. She reads a letter from the man who murdered her brother. He has consented to a visit, but she wonders why. What is going on in his head? Has he become a hardened criminal? Is there any humanity left in him? Will he only glare at her pitilessly as she pours out her heart, refusing to admit guilt and express sympathy, coldly satisfied that the misery he inflicted so many years ago continues?

Sunday received visitation rights in record time. Her husband drove her to the prison four hours away. They exchanged few words during those hours in the car, as if silence was the only word that could be spoken. On arrival, Sunday continued on into the prison by herself—this was her business, and hers alone.

As she walked through that first security door, her mind drifted back to her brother. She felt flooded with memories, longing, and love. She missed him intensely. She thought of all those lost years and all the suffering—the life of the brother she loved cut so short, a wife and children left behind, so devastated by the loss, a family traumatized and bewildered by such a senseless act of violence.

The loud clang of the security door behind her jarred her thoughts back to the present. Once she was searched and cleared by a guard, she made her way to the visitation room. She walked through one steel door after another, down one long corridor after another, as if entering into the bowels of some dark and dangerous place, an earthly purgatory. Surprisingly, there was no more sadness in her, no anger or revenge, no fear. She was ready to meet the man who had murdered her brother.

A deputy ushered her to a table in a corner of the visitation room. There she sat in prayerful silence. After several minutes, she heard a steel door open and, turning around, looked for the first time into the face of the man who had killed her brother. She stood up, walked over to him, and, taking his trembling hand, greeted him warmly. At that moment she was filled with nothing but feelings of emotion and pity for the broken and terrified man who stood before her, his head bowed in shame. They talked briefly. He expressed his regret and apologized for the wrong he had done and the suffering he had caused.

Then Sunday delivered her two messages from God. "God loves you so much," she told Fred, "that he sent Jesus to die for you." And then, "It is not too late to become the man that God designed you to be." The conversation continued for a long time. In the course of that conversation, Sunday witnessed a miracle. Before her very eyes, Fred committed his life to Jesus Christ. Sunday eventually had to leave the prison, which proved to be especially difficult. After all, who would want to leave the scene of a miracle? But the relationship did not stop then and there. Sunday and Fred have exchanged letters ever since and have become warm friends.

I was astonished when I first read her story. It lingered in my mind for a long time. What inspired this woman to reach out to the man who murdered her brother? Where did she get the courage? How did she find the words? According to the story she told me, it was God who inspired her, God who filled her with courage, God who gave her the words.

I also think about the message God told her to deliver. The first part fits my Christian beliefs perfectly. Considering the biblical story, how could anyone dispute it? God loves Fred—God loves all of us—and sent Jesus to die for us to accomplish our salvation. My eyes well up with tears when I think about it, for it reminds me of my own conversion. God loves sinners, which is why Jesus came as a human being, suffered, died, and rose from the grave, thus conquering death itself. No one is beyond the reach of the grace of God—not the thief on the cross, not cowardly Peter or murderous Paul or demon-possessed Mary. Not even Fred, who sits in a California prison. Christ's saving birth, death, and resurrection apply to all—no exceptions.

It is the second message that strikes me as more puzzling, even troubling. "It is not too late to become the man that God designed you to be." It sounds appealing, to be sure; it tugs on the heart. But is it really true? Some people seem to have the time, capacity, and opportunity to become the people God wants them to be. But not everyone. Is it true for the elderly or the disabled or infirm? For people who have suffered severe losses? For people like Fred, who face circumstances so severe and miserable that it seems almost impossible for good to come to them or out of them. Doesn't Sunday's message awaken expectations that simply can't be fulfilled?

"Tell Fred that it is not too late to become the man that I designed him to be." But it does seem too late for Fred.

Then again, maybe not.

Here is the paradox of the Christian faith. The two messages Sunday delivered to Fred are both true — the second being true because the first is true. In fact, the two messages are true because they are really one message. Jesus Christ died for the sins of the world. This is the reason Fred can become the man God designed him to be. In fact, he already is that man — new, perfect, and complete — though he still has a long way to go. New yet still being made new, perfect yet still growing toward perfection, complete yet still experiencing completion strikes the right tension. It is exactly what redemption means.

Redemption

The word *redemption* can be grouped with a larger family of English words that for the most part begin with the prefix *re-*, which denotes an original state of affairs, something that once was, a condition that used to prevail and can be returned to. But an original—and presumably preferred—state of affairs also implies some kind of departure, decline, degradation, or deterioration. Consequently, the *re-* indicates movement back to something—from bad back to good, from sickness back to health, from crooked back to straight.

Once you grasp this essential feature of the prefix, words that use it make more sense. We *re*store an old, rusty beater to mint condition, like it used to be when it was first driven off the assembly line, and we *re*build a shed that was ready to collapse from neglect and disuse. We *re*sume class after winter break, which gets us back into our normal routine. We *re*turn to a pathway from which we wandered for a while, and so continue where we left off. We *re*visit an idea we had once discarded and *re*consider whether it might work after all. We *re*claim a house we lost to bankruptcy, *re*new a relationship that faded over time, *re*cover health after a long illness, and *re*concile former enemies, making them friends. We *re*form corrupt institutions so they once again uphold the purpose for which they were established. We experience a *re*birth of interest in some hobby we lost passion for. We *re*discover the pleasure of a family lake cabin we didn't visit for many years because we were too busy advancing our careers. Every one of these words implies going back to an original—perhaps even ideal—condition that was lost.

*Re*demption follows the same logic, but with an important theological twist. We redeem someone who is bound, captive, enslaved, held hostage, which results in a condition that is much better than the original. Unlike other *re*-words, therefore, redemption has a future orientation that is grounded in God's eternal purpose, which is to make us his own. It implies deliverance, to be sure, but also liberation and ultimate victory. A slave is redeemed, set free to become a productive citizen; a prisoner is released from confinement and makes a significant contribution to society; a hostage is returned to his home country and ends up playing a prominent role in it. Redemption, however, always has a cost attached to it, which we call a ransom — a sum of money, an exchange of prisoners, an offering of territory. In every case, something of value must be exchanged, some payment made.

It could even cost a life. In Charles Dickens's *A Tale of Two Cities*, for example, one man takes the place of another and heroically dies for him, and no one notices because they look so much alike. Likewise, in the novel *A Thousand Splendid Suns*, an older woman, Miriam, dies for a younger friend in order to allow her to flee Afghanistan with her husband and build a new life in another country. In C. S. Lewis's classic *The Lion, the Witch, and the Wardrobe*, the lion, Aslan, provides the ransom by dying in place of the traitor Edmund.

The Christian faith teaches that every human being is a slave to sin and destined to die, thus suffering eternal separation from God. Jesus Christ, God's Son, became the ransom, setting humanity free from such a horrible fate. Paul states it this way: "There is no difference between Jew and Gentile, for all have sinned and fall short of the glory of God, and

only through faith

all are justified freely by his grace through the redemption that came by Christ Jesus. God presented Christ as a sacrifice of atonement, through the shedding of his blood—to be received by faith" (Romans 3:22b–25a). Likewise, Paul writes in his letter to the church in Ephesus, "In him we have redemption through his blood, the forgiveness of sins, in accordance with the riches of God's grace that he lavished on us" (Ephesians 1:7–8a).

Redemption *from* something—namely, sin and death and hell—also implies redemption *for* something, which once again points to the future. Redemption promises reconciliation between God and humanity, thereby turning enmity into friendship; restoring our broken relationship with God; repairing the divine image in us, once marred almost beyond recognition; renewing spiritual lives that were selfish, stagnant, and perverse; reforming ugly character and conduct; and resurrecting the body after death, which will make our bodies fit for eternity. God reclaims what is rightfully his. He created us; he redeemed us. We belong to him, twice over. In short, we are not only liberated from sin and evil, we are also given new life—a life so new that the apostle Paul equates it with sharing in the inexpressible and inexhaustible glory of God.

THE PRISONERS

I discovered just how stunning the promise of redemption is during a trip to Italy in my early twenties. I visited the city of Florence the summer after I graduated from college, newly married and bound for seminary in the fall. Florence is an attractive tourist spot because it contains a rich treasure of renaissance art, all within easy and convenient walking distance. We had planned our visit carefully. There was one gallery in particular my wife and I wanted to visit. In fact, it was the first one on our list, for the Galleria dell'Accademia displays one piece of art we wanted to see more than any other—Michelangelo's famous sculpture of David.

We were not disappointed. Standing atop a pedestal, the marble sculpture towered above us, rising some twenty feet from the gallery floor. We were stunned by its enormity, beauty, and perfection. There David stood, silently looming over us, his body tall and erect, his face calm and alert, one hand holding a slingshot slung over his muscular shoulder, the other hanging at his side, grasping a smooth stone. He appeared to be gazing intensely at Goliath. Art historians don't know whether Michelangelo's David had already defeated Goliath or was about to fight him. Once we gazed at the sculpture, it didn't seem to matter much. Either way, David exuded such serene and quiet confidence that, whether Goliath was alive or already dead, he knew long before the battle that Goliath was his. David symbolizes the glorification of a man made in the image of God.

We did not know, however, that the gallery housed other works of art as well, including five sculptures that Michelangelo never completed. Called "Prisoners," these unfinished sculptures consist of figures partially encased in marble.

What makes them so startling and compelling is that the finished parts of them are perfect. In one, it is an arm and torso and face; in another, the entire front of a man's body; in yet another, shoulders, chest, stomach, and one leg, all exhibiting the fine and intricate features, smoothly finished, of a human body not yet complete. Each sculpture pulsates with a strange kind of energy too, as if the figure is straining against the marble, trying to climb out to gain its freedom. Hence the title "Prisoners." The marble appears to be holding them captive, and the unfinished figures are striving to escape.

Michelangelo believed that he, a sculptor of stone, was a tool in the hands of God, assigned the task of releasing his subjects from the marble that entombed them. He was so intent on fulfilling this mission that he often worked himself into a frenzied state, as if possessed by divine power.

Michelangelo's vision of David was remarkably, almost supernaturally clear. He had the capacity to see a figure hidden within the marble even before he started to sculpt. It was as if the figure already existed and Michelangelo simply had to remove the excess stone that held it captive. Unlike most sculptors of his day, who first formed a plaster model and then marked a block of marble to approximate what they hoped to create, Michelangelo worked freehand—no pattern, no model, no markings. This allowed him to start in at any point in the marble, which was usually somewhere in the middle, and to expand outward from there. Moreover, he sculpted to perfection wherever he happened to start, which gives the impression that the figure — half finished, half unfinished — was trying to claw and crawl its way out; an obviously impossible task, since only Michelangelo had the power to set it free.

These "prisoners" can teach us something about the Christian faith. God is the artist; we are the sculptures. God has created us and redeemed us. He sees us, knows us, loves us, delights in us. He has made us new creations in Jesus Christ. We have nothing to do or add to what God has already done. His work is complete and finished.

But here's the problem. As perfect as we are, we are still stuck in marble, still held prisoner by bad habits and ugly thoughts and sinful behaviors. We don't always act, think, or feel anything like the new and perfect person we are, as I discovered after my conversion at the age of twenty — a prodigal returned home, who still brought home with him the world he had tried to leave behind.

There is work yet to be done, excess marble yet to be removed. Thus, as God's perfect works of art, we are new in Christ, yet still being made new, redeemed yet still needing redemption, finished yet still emerging. God has only begun to transform us, though we are already transformed; his Spirit has only gotten started, though we are complete. We have a glorious future ahead of us, and we can move into that future with confidence and security.

What we are now in Christ we must yet become. This requires a story and a setting, which is where we turn next.

CHAPTER 3

A Story in Search
of Characters

Call me sentimental if you wish. But here I am, at the age of sixty, reading *The Chronicles of Narnia* aloud for the fifth time. I read the series to each of my children when they were young, then again to all of them when they were older (my daughter thought it would be a good family activity before she headed off to college). Now I am reading them to my new wife, Patricia. Once again, I have ended up doing all the reading—by her request, I should add. Patricia says she likes the way I do the different voices, no doubt because I have practiced them for so long. The character of Puddle-glum, a Marsh-wiggle, has always been my favorite, and the voice I imagine him to have provides a grand opportunity to be a little histrionic.

Reading stories has long been a family tradition. Over the years I have read hundreds of books to my kids, and they have continued the tradition on their own. My daughter and son-in-law have already made their way through the entire Harry Potter series and the Lord of the Rings trilogy, all in the last two years. They have become as addicted as I am. I suspect my sons will follow suit. In the process, my children have gained an appreciation for story itself, which has helped them, I think, understand the world and their place in it.

We keep returning to the great authors, like George McDonald, J. R. R. Tolkien, and C. S. Lewis, time and time again. I have often pondered what makes their stories so captivating and moving. Just last night, for example, I had to pause when reading *The Magician's Nephew* because my eyes welled up with tears. A boy named Digory is distressed because he thinks the time is past and opportunity wasted to appeal to Aslan to heal his sickly mother. Quite unintentionally, he finally blurts out what has long been simmering in his heart, and at the most inopportune time. Feeling exposed and ashamed, Digory keeps his eyes down, fixed on Aslan's paws. But then, as if compelled by the force of Aslan's royal presence, he slowly raises his eyes to look into Aslan's face. He expects to see Aslan glaring at him in anger, a magnifying glass burning a hole into his heart, for he knows how grievous his wrongdoing has been, how catastrophic the consequences of letting a witch into the newly born world of Narnia. Much to his surprise, however, he sees tears in Aslan's eyes, giant tears that almost threaten to drown him. In that moment he discovers that Aslan is more than ferocious; he is also compassionate.

Story as Truth

What makes stories like The Chronicles of Narnia so good, and why do they keep winning new generations of readers decades, even centuries, after they were written? There are the obvious reasons, of course. They use lively language, develop compelling characters, and move the plot along at a steady pace. But I think there is another — and deeper — reason. The best stories are good, standing the test of time, because they reflect another, bigger and better story, the biblical story. And the biblical story is good because it is true — so true, in fact, that it is simply Truth. The biblical story illumines all other and lesser stories, making them come to life as a sunrise lights up the world. These lesser stories are derivative — true to the degree that they are grounded in Truth, true in the same way color is real because light exists.

Sometimes the obvious yet overlooked truths — those we tend to assume as commonplace — are the most profound. They are so deep they might at first appear shallow, like the bottom of a crystal clear lake that plunges to a depth far deeper than we think. Surely this is the case with the biblical story. That it is a story hardly deserves mentioning. Most of us have grown up reading the great stories of the Bible, like the stories of Joseph and Esther and Samson and, of course, Jesus. We know the plots and characters, but we haven't necessarily thought much about the fact that story itself is central to the Christian faith.

The Christian faith is not, therefore, something else.

For example, it is not in essence a set of moral principles or laws — though it does reveal certain moral codes, like the Ten Commandments and the Sermon on the Mount, which are contained within a larger story arc that tells us who God is and how he works in the world. Christianity is no more a set of laws than a sport can be reduced to a set of rules. Rules provide the guidelines; the sport puts us on the court or in the pool or on the field, where the action is. We must learn to follow the rules, of course; but the sport is different from the rules because it is the real thing. Besides, laws only tell us how to live right; the Christian faith shows us what God has done to make us right.

Neither is the Christian faith in essence a system of theology. Philosophers and theologians explain the Christian faith, to be sure, condensing its teachings and stories into a clear, concise, and logical system. But theological reflection about the Christian story is not the story itself, any more than a map of a place is the actual place — London or New Zealand or Yellowstone National Park. The biblical story is primary; theological reflection, however necessary and important, is secondary. Theology tells us how to think and what to believe; the biblical story provides the actual content of belief because it describes how God has acted in the world. Theology is an abstraction; the biblical story is real, not as a photograph of a person is real, not as the verbal description of a person is real, but as an actual person is real.

Nor is the Christian faith the same as the religious culture that it sometimes produces. We say of Western Europe and the United States that these are "Christian nations" with a population that claims Christianity as its primary belief system. The vast majority of this population is familiar with Christian beliefs and rituals as well. But such familiarity is more the result of birth and background, of broad cultural influence, than it is of genuine faith in the gospel and obedience to God's commands. Watching a movie does not make one an actor; eating good food does not make one a chef. Growing up in a Christian culture, broadly speaking, does not make one a real Christian.

Finally, the Christian faith is not reducible to a mystical experience, though over the centuries many Christians have had mystical experiences, often so ineffable that they have not been able to say much about them, which was true even of the apostle Paul (2 Corinthians 12:1–10). When they try to describe them, they use language that makes these experiences seem incomprehensible, which they probably are. Mystical experiences are so personal, so mysterious, and so idiosyncratic that language simply fails. Words like "awareness" and "being" and "mindfulness" and "enlightenment" sound impressively, deeply religious, but they are also highly subjective and hard to understand, like trying to grasp the light of the sun with our bare hands. The individual soul might achieve enlightenment, but everyone else can say little more than, "Wow! So happy for you." The biblical story, however, is as concrete and specific as Samson's long hair, Rahab's house of prostitution, Paul's forty lashes less one, and Lydia's purple dye business. Stories traffic in the stuff of real people living in actual places and doing concrete actions. Mysticism points from earth to Heaven; the biblical story tells how Heaven came to earth and entered into the messy world of people.

Many religions contain stories, of course, but these stories are subservient to something else, like laws or philosophy or mysticism. The Christian faith is different because it is story from start to finish. This grand story—*his*-story, really—shows that human history is the primary arena of God's action. It is God who not only invented history but also got involved in it—to the point that he showed up in person.

That the Christian faith is story might not strike you as all that significant, at least not at first. But there is a reason why it really is important—so important, in fact, that it could change your life. It certainly did mine. Though it might seem to consist of little more than a series of random events, with no plot or theme or meaning to them, your life is in fact a story. And knowing the biblical story might help you understand your story better, making sense of it when it doesn't seem to make much sense. As I will explain later, such was the experience I had in the wake of the accident. But before I return to that story, I want to explore the bigger story of the Bible.

THE BIG STORY

The plotline of this story is clear enough. God created the world out of nothing, and he created it good. Each day of his creation set the stage for the next, until God was ready to finish it all with his last and best act, the creation of human beings. He made them male and female and charged them to be fruitful and multiply, to subdue the earth (which means to cultivate it and care for it, not exploit it), and to trust and obey him, their Creator. They were also given a garden—a bountiful and beautiful place in which humans could work, love, and flourish.

As the story unfolds, the first two humans, Adam and Eve, chose to rebel and assert themselves against God, denying that they were mere creatures, finite and fragile, utterly dependent on God for their very existence. This act of rebellion depicts how evil came into the world, and it set off a chain reaction of evil that sent the entire world into a downward spiral of brokenness and suffering, making all subsequent generations selfish, alienated, lonely, bewildered, and broken. The first few chapters of Genesis tell us that Adam and Eve hid from God, blamed each other, and began to face hardship in the world. Their hard hearts turned toward darkness. Banished from the garden, they fell from their position of privilege and security and became nomads on earth.

But the downward spiral did not stop there. The sad story continues, telling us that one of their sons killed the other in a jealous rage; clans and tribes and nations warred against each other; culture itself became base and corrupt. Swollen with arrogance, the human race, wishing to make a "name" for itself, tried to build a tower that would reach to the heavens in a vain attempt to push God out of his own domain. God had little choice but to scatter them over the face of the earth.

But God was not about to give up, however dark and bleak the world had become. He set in motion a redemptive plan—a plan that would span centuries and continents—to make right what had gone so wrong. Surprisingly, the first concrete step to fulfill this great plan was an inauspiciously small one. God called to himself one couple, Abraham and Sarah. He made a promise to bless them, to give them a great name, and to use them to bless the world. In exchange, he asked them to trust him, which they did (with a few regrettable slips along the way). Abraham and Sarah eventually had a child, Isaac, who carried on God's redemptive plan into the second generation; their children did the same into the third generation. Soon a family grew to be a clan; over time that clan turned into a tribe, known as the Hebrews; many centuries later that tribe became the nation of Israel.

Abraham's descendants settled in the Promised Land for a time. A famine forced them to migrate south into Egypt, where, after enjoying protection under Joseph for a generation, they eventually became slaves. After several hundred years, God called Moses to lead his people out of Egypt, delivering them from slavery and back to the Promised Land. During the exodus, God performed ten signs, parted the Red Sea, and provided food, water, and protection for them in the wilderness. He also gave them a law — the Ten Commandments — to show them how to trust and obey him. Such acts of divine mercy should have been enough to demonstrate that God intended to fulfill his promise to bless his people, and through them to bless the world. Strangely, the more God did, performing miracles for them and providing for their needs, the more they rebelled against him, as if mercy made them mean, goodness and generosity made them greedy.

Joshua eventually led God's people into the Promised Land, which they gradually — and incompletely — conquered. God warned them to avoid mingling with local tribes and flirting with local religions, which were corrupt to the core. But they ignored his warning, spurned his presence, and disobeyed his law. So God gave them up to their enemies, allowing them to suffer the consequences of rebellion. After suffering years of subjugation, they cried out to God, and God sent a deliverer (known as a "judge") to save them. Time and time again this pattern was repeated. But they never seemed to learn. The reason was simple enough, a reason that should strike a familiar chord with us: they chose self-rule over God's rule, self-interest over obedience.

Weary of the cycle, the people began to clamor for a king, whom they believed would not only make them free, but also give them power to dominate the nations around them. God granted their request, but not before warning them of the consequences that would surely follow. Three kings — Saul, David, and Solomon — ruled in succession before the empire of Israel split in two. As two separate kingdoms — Israel in the north and Judah in the south — they declared war on each other, brother fighting brother, family warring against family. God sent prophets to warn them of judgment, but the people — his people, we must remember — refused to listen. In time, both kingdoms were conquered by foreign powers, the north by the Assyrians, the south by the Babylonians.

Still, the redemptive story was not over, for God would

not let it be over. It continued to unfold through Judah, the southern kingdom. Some seventy years after the Babylonian conquest, a small group of captives returned to the Promised Land. They rebuilt the walls of Jerusalem and the temple. They also did their best to keep themselves pure by separating from the peoples that surrounded them, friends as well as enemies. As it turned out, such radical separation kept them from doing what God had willed from the very beginning, to be a blessing to all people, a light to the nations.

Nothing seemed to work. The law did not make God's people obedient; the Promised Land did not keep them from compromise; the sacrificial system did not inspire or impart holiness of life; the temple did not keep worship pure; prophets, priests, and kings did not engender justice and righteousness. The promise God had made to Abraham and Sarah kept waiting for fulfillment, like a story in search of a good ending. Every episode along the way — failure and repentance, conquest and return, disappointment and renewal — pointed ahead, toward something that was yet to come, awakening a hope for fulfillment.

Finally, God himself came as a real human being, incarnated as Jesus Christ. Jesus was born to a virgin in a stable, was reared in a small town, and practiced the trade of a common laborer. He grew up in a traditional Jewish home, studied the Torah, and attended the synagogue. Yet he was different, too — human, to be sure, but somehow other. He was the Messiah and Son of God, sent on a special mission to fulfill the promise to Abraham and Sarah. He healed the sick, cast out demons, announced good news to the poor and disenfranchised, and taught with authority.

Surprisingly, his ministry resulted in a gruesome death. He accomplished his special mission in a way no Jew could have imagined—not by wielding a sword, not by playing the role of a holy man, not by gaining wealth and privilege, not by performing miracles, not by amassing political power, but by suffering and dying for the sins of the world. In the end, his own people—God's people, the recipients of the promise to Abraham and Sarah—called for his death, and Roman soldiers, carrying out the will of the most sophisticated empire on earth, executed him by nailing him to a cross, a crude and brutal form of execution.

The story could have—and would have—ended right there, if Jesus had remained in the grave. But three days later he rose from the dead, thus conquering death itself and proving that the greatest enemy people face—their own sin —had been finally defeated. He appeared to his followers on many occasions after the resurrection and, just before returning to his Father in Heaven, sent them forth to proclaim the good news of salvation and to do the work of the kingdom. Within one generation, those disciples fanned out across the Roman world, winning converts, making disciples, and planting churches in dozens of cities. By the end of the biblical story they had expanded well beyond Jerusalem all the way to Rome, the capital of the Western world.

It is a wonderful story. There is grandeur to it, drama and intrigue, heroism and villainy, tragedy and incredible triumph. The story, breathtaking in its scope, reaches across centuries and continents and empires. It is like a vast mountain range that stretches out before us. Still, no story, not even the biblical story, is merely big. A huge landscape always consists of a thousand little scenes—hills, lakes, trees, canyons, cliffs, streams, and meadows. The big story of redemption is made up of lots of little stories, often involving unnamed and unknown people living in small corners of the world doing good deeds that hardly seem worthy of notice.

We see the scope of the biblical story unfold before us, situated, as we are, some two thousand years after it ended. But the characters we read about did not have the vantage point we have now because they were *inside* the story. There is so much they did not know, so much they could not see. They were as ignorant and confused as a detective at the beginning of a mystery novel. Like that detective, they had to piece together various clues that seemed more confusing than clarifying. Still, they chose to believe that their lives were caught up in a bigger story. They chose to trust God and follow him into an unknown future, however slim the evidence of a bigger story that could make sense out of their little ones.

A LITTLE STORY

The story of Ruth provides a useful illustration of what it means to make sense of a little story hidden within a bigger story. Few Old Testament stories weave the two kinds of stories together so powerfully—and few demonstrate how a little story can so dramatically contribute to the fulfillment of the bigger story of redemption.

The setting is Bethlehem during the chaotic period of the judges when, as the writer of Judges tells us, people did what was right in their own eyes. In the opening scene we meet Naomi, her husband, and her two sons, who leave Bethlehem to escape a terrible famine. They travel to a foreign country, Moab, a small and prosperous nation then on friendly terms with Israel, where they settle down to build a life. Eventually, Naomi's husband dies, but she is spared from poverty because her sons marry women from Moab and continue to care for her, as good sons in that culture were expected to do.

Then tragedy strikes again, this time more brutally. Naomi loses both her sons, which leaves her utterly destitute. Desperate to survive, she decides to return to Bethlehem, hoping that distant relatives will take her in. She tells her two daughters-in-law, Orpah and Ruth, to remain in Moab, where their prospects for survival — marriage, in other words — are better. Both Orpah and Ruth follow Naomi as she begins to make her way home. However, at the border, Naomi again urges them to return to their homes, country, and kin. Orpah decides to turn back, but Ruth remains at Naomi's side, clinging to her and promising loyalty in words we now sometimes use in wedding liturgies:

> Do not press me to leave you
> or to turn back from following you!
> Where you go, I will go;

where you lodge, I will lodge;
your people shall be my people,
and your God my God.
Where you die, I will die—
there will I be buried.
May the Lord do thus and so to me,
and more as well,
if even death parts me from you!

(Ruth 1:16–17 NRSV)

Thus, Naomi and Ruth, mother and daughter-in-law, widow and foreigner, forsaken, bereft, and poor, return to Bethlehem. Upon their arrival, friends and neighbors express shock at their misfortune. Naomi is so distraught by her losses that she tells her friends to call her Mara instead of Naomi, for Mara means "bitter." "I went away full," she says, "but the LORD has brought me back empty. Why call me Naomi? The LORD has afflicted me; the Almighty has brought misfortune upon me" (Ruth 1:21).

But Ruth proves that she is as resourceful as she is loyal. Desperate for food, she begins to glean grain in the field of one of Naomi's distant relatives. This relative, Boaz, a wealthy landowner and leading citizen of the community, notices Ruth and inquires about her. Upon meeting her, he declares what has become common knowledge in the community:

I've been told all about what you have done for your mother-in-law since the death of your husband—how you left your father and mother and your homeland and came to live with a people you did not know before.

May the Lord repay you for what you have done. May you be richly rewarded by the Lord, the God of Israel, under whose wings you have come to take refuge. (Ruth 2:11–12)

Boaz invites her to continue gleaning in his fields for the rest of harvest season and orders his foremen to protect her from molestation, which only underscores the moral chaos that permeated the culture of that day.

At the end of the harvest season, Naomi recognizes that the favor Boaz has shown to Ruth means he might be willing to offer his protection, which implies doing what next of kin was obligated by custom to do—marry the widow of a dead relative in order to continue the family name. Boaz realizes, however, that another man living in the community is closer kin, and so the first choice is his. Boaz meets the man at the city gate, and witnesses gather. The man is eager to acquire Naomi's property, assuming it will become his. But when he learns that he must marry Ruth, carry on the family name that belongs to her, and pass on Naomi's inheritance to Ruth's children rather than to his own, he refuses. He's not interested in a marriage that would impose responsibility but provide no material benefit. "I cannot redeem it," he says, "because I might endanger my own estate" (Ruth 4:6). So Boaz steps forward to fulfill his duty and honors Ruth for the sacrifice she is making. "The Lord bless you, my daughter ...This kindness is greater than that which you showed earlier: You have not run after the younger men, whether rich or poor" (Ruth 3:10).

Ruth and Boaz marry. In due time, Ruth conceives and gives birth to a son. The women of the community, functioning like a Greek chorus, celebrate the happy ending to Ruth and Naomi's difficult story and praise the God who has been involved in the entire plot. They say to Naomi, "He will renew your life and sustain you in your old age. For your daughter-in-law, who loves you and who is better to you than seven sons, has given him birth" (Ruth 4:15).

It is a good story, and it ends well, like most good stories do. Boaz gets a son, though he must rear him to preserve another man's name and heritage; Ruth marries and gets a family, though her husband is a generation older; Naomi finds comfort and solace in her old age, though she has suffered many losses along the way. But the story itself hardly seems significant. Why is it worthy of preservation and honor? Bethlehem is a small town, far removed from the center of civilization; Naomi and Boaz belong to a small tribe; Ruth is a refugee who settles in a foreign land. It is parochial, quaint, and charming, a nice bedtime story that entertains, inspires, and comforts. In short, it has all the appearance of being nothing more than a "little" story, which appears to be the case with our stories as well.

Little Merged into Big

But there is more to the story than meets the eye. Ruth names her son Obed, who eventually grows up, marries, and has children of his own. Obed names one of his sons Jesse.

When Jesse grows up, he also marries and has eight sons, the youngest of whom is named David, who just happens to become the greatest king in Israel's history. Of course, Boaz and Ruth have long since passed from the scene by the time David is born. They have no idea how their story, a story of tragedy and sacrifice and loyalty, continues to unfold over time, culminating in David's rise to power.

Even so, the story is still not finished. Many generations later, another son is born, a descendent of Naomi the widow, of Ruth the foreigner, and of Boaz the landowner — characters whose lives were woven together in a small Judean town during the period of the judges. This son's name is Jesus, the Son of God and Savior of the world. It seems Ruth's little story turned out to be very big indeed. Naomi's words to Ruth — "wait, my daughter, until you find out what happens" (Ruth 3:18) — were far more prophetic than she could have imagined.

There is no way Ruth could have known what would happen in the decades and centuries that followed her short time on earth. She was simply blind to it, her vision confined by her immediate circumstances, which is true for all of us, bound, as we are, by time. We know more than Ruth did, of course, for our stories come much later, which means that we know what happened in the decades and centuries that followed, including how her story culminated in the birth of Jesus. Still, we are blinded by our immediate circumstances too, just as she was, which makes it exceedingly difficult for us to see and believe how each of our stories fit into the big story. It is hard to see much of anything when consumed by pain, anguish, and doubt.

Nevertheless, little stories continue to unfold, contributing to the big redemptive story, though there is no way we can know how, at least not yet. Friends of mine recently adopted a boy from China, their story thus merging with his. Who knows what will happen to Ben as a result? An entrepreneur living in the Middle East has started three schools that attract not only Christian students but also Muslim students, some of whom have become Christians. What great feats might those converts accomplish in the years ahead? My own son-in-law, Jacob, founded an orphanage in Bogota, Columbia, for girls from highly traumatized backgrounds; a local church is now running it, largely through volunteers. What might happen to those girls who, once so deprived, are now being loved and provided for in the name of Jesus? These stories remind us that God's work of redemption continues. God is using ordinary people to make the world whole and healthy again.

I wonder how that might be true—or better put, will be true—for you and me? How might the little story of my life and your life contribute to the bigger story of the world's redemption? It is hard to see from day to day, largely because our own stories seem so trivial, meaningless, or random. We race through life, enduring tragedy, laboring on the job or at home, doing routine tasks, often so distracted by pressures and responsibilities that we lack the time, energy, or even interest to think much about the possible significance of our life story. We seem like workers on an assembly line who have forgotten to consider the high-end product we are helping to make.

CHORUS OF BIBLICAL VOICES

Knowing the biblical story might help us make better sense of our own little stories, provided we read and interpret our stories in light of *the* story. When I think back to twenty years ago, a vivid and terrifying memory comes to my mind. I am riding in an emergency vehicle. My children are with me, whimpering quietly. We are all aching with pain, utterly bewildered, trembling with the shock of having just witnessed the death of wife and mother, daughter and sister, mother and grandmother. We are driving down a lonely stretch of highway, headed toward a hospital some fifty miles away. All is silence in the emergency vehicle; it is a heavy silence full of sadness and confusion and fear. But in that silence I begin to hear a familiar echo in my head, faint but clear, like the roll of distant thunder. Listening as carefully as I can, I realize the echo is the sound of biblical texts that keep bouncing off the walls of my mind, one after the other, calling out to me:

You intended to harm me, but God intended it for good. (Genesis 50:20)

And who knows but that you have come to your royal position for such a time as this? (Esther 4:14)

- *We know that in all things God works for the good of those who love him, who have been called according to his purpose.* (Romans 8:28)

- *My Father, if it is possible, may this cup be taken from me. Yet not as I will, but as you will.* (Matthew 26:39)

- *Teach us to number our days, that we may gain a heart of wisdom.* (Psalm 90:12)

Echo after echo, like a chorus of biblical voices. Sitting in the ambulance, I discover that the tragic story into which we have been thrust is enveloped by another story. The accident, however random, does not stand on its own or exist unto itself. It is part of a larger story. In that moment, I have no idea how; that is for me to discover in the future. For now, in the painful silence, it is enough to know there is a story out there that can make sense of my own. But it is not merely *a* story; it is *the* story.

OUR STORIES IN LIGHT OF *THE* STORY

Knowing the biblical story will not solve every problem or answer every question you may have, any more than it has solved all of my problems and answered all of my questions. It will not always make decisions obvious or life comfortable and easy. It will not relieve you of all pain, temptation, struggle, doubt, and discouragement. It will not spare you from suffering or deliver you from the misery of living in a fallen world. But it will provide perspective, a foundation for faith, and a vision of hope. It will help you to believe that the story of your life does not consist of a series of random, disconnected events that have no meaning or purpose. A bigger story of redemption is unfolding, and it will help you to make sense of your own.

Consider a few scenarios you might face:

- You find yourself in a situation that calls for an act of courage that puts your safety at risk. You remind yourself in that moment that Esther faced just those circumstances many centuries ago. It was her cousin Mordecai who challenged her with words that still ring true: "And who knows but that you have come to your royal position for such a time as this?"

- You sense God calling you to sacrifice your time and resources to help a person who might best be described as difficult to love—driven to self-destructive behavior and unconcerned about his impact on anyone else. You call to mind Jesus' experience of abandonment in the garden of Gethsemane, and you repeat the prayer he uttered in the face of his impending death: "Not as I will, but as you will."

- You endure years of suffering, some of it your own fault, some of it not. You remember the story of Joseph—his betrayal, his long years of enslavement and imprisonment—and his immortal words come to your mind: "You intended to harm me, but God intended it for good."

- You face an overwhelmingly difficult task for which you feel completely inadequate. The story of Ezra and Nehemiah, who, facing fierce opposition, were called to rebuild Jerusalem after the exile, reminds you that others have faced similar circumstances and, by prayer and persistence and wisdom, triumphed.

- You agonize over a choice between two options —one is clearly better for you but the other is better for someone else. Neither option is clearly right or wrong. In that moment, you remember Ruth's predicament, her courageous choice, and its incredible outcome.

Disciplined reflection

Reflecting on your story this way requires discipline. You will have to give it time, devote yourself to prayer, exercise discernment, and perhaps seek the counsel of others. It's unlikely you will learn much, at least not right away. But over time, you might start to pick up and follow a narrative thread of redemption running through your life, one that helps you to understand your story in light of *the* story and to feel a surge of energy as you move into a future that is rich with meaning.

In the aftermath of the accident, sitting alone night after night in the dark with my children tucked snugly into bed, that chorus of biblical voices kept speaking to me. Sometimes they spoke loudly, sometimes faintly: *We lived in the same world you do, Jerry. We experienced the same hardships and felt the same loneliness and faced the same doubts. Remember our stories and consider how they ended. Your story will be no different, nor will your children's. Remember our stories.*

And remember is what I tried to do, using my imagination to get inside their stories so I could feel them as well as think them. When I pondered the mystery of my own story, I began to believe, if just a little, that perhaps it might fit and perhaps did fit into some larger narrative of redemption.

"All things are yours," Paul told the Corinthians. The entire biblical story is at your disposal to inform and illumine and inspire you to stay on course—the course of faith, hope, and love—no matter what your circumstances happen to be. It is a redemptive story, and it is still unfolding. Now, as always, that story is searching for characters who are willing to step forward to play a role. As it turns out, people like you and me, however little our stories seem to be, can play a much bigger role than we think. Remember Ruth, a foreign Moabite, who was grafted into the family that produced the Savior of the world. If she only knew! That might very well be said of us someday, too. "If they only knew!"

CHAPTER 4

Scene and Setting

Scene and setting are like props on a stage; they provide the material conditions for a story to unfold. No story takes place in a vacuum; it always requires a context. Pick up any novel and read a few pages. You will be drawn almost immediately into a scene and setting that serve as the backdrop for the main plot of the story—sometimes beautiful and serene, sometimes ugly and riotous. Scene and setting do not always have the sun shining through a window on a lovely spring morning.

In fact, rarely is the scene and setting of life perfect. My wife, Patricia, works as both a nurse and a licensed mental health therapist. Reflecting on a typical day, she often comments that a whole lot of people in this world face adversity, much of it harsh and grueling. Some triumph; others flounder. But whether they emerge the victor or remain a victim, the fact remains that they suffer under circumstances no one would ever choose. These circumstances don't consist of a bad day occurring every so often over the course of a lifetime but of one bad day followed by another bad day with unrelenting ferocity. Each day they wake up to the same pain, the same disease, the same hard marriage, the same wayward children, the same mental illness, or the same corrosive poverty they had to endure the day before. Day in, day out, it is always more of the same.

Our Inheritance — for Good or Ill

The story of Adam and Eve begins with a perfect world. That world has long since disappeared; there is no more new and perfect world, no more clean slate. Every member of the human race has entered a story already well underway and assumed a role already assigned to them. Among other things, we have all inherited a gene pool, a body type, tendencies and talents, pedigree and parentage, burdens and opportunities. We have freedom, to be sure; but it is limited all the same, sometimes severely. We have options, but not an infinite number of options. It is a mystery to me how it all works, why life turns out the way it does — for one person so happily, for another so harshly.

Sometimes in morning silence I wonder why I entered the story when I did, where I did, and how I did. Why was I born as an American in the second half of the twentieth century? Why not as a European Jew in 1933? Why into a home with a good and godly mother? Why not into a home with no mother at all? Why with expectations and opportunities to use my gifts for the greater good of society? Why not with little expectation and opportunity? Why with a healthy body and sound mind? Why not with schizophrenia or cerebral palsy? I simply cannot answer these questions. The storyline I inherited at birth is a fact, a given. I suppose I could attribute it to fate, as many people do. I could also attribute it to the sovereign plan of God, which is what I choose to do. Still, whether the result of accident or providence, the story of my life did not begin at my birth, and it will not end at my death either.

This leads to another mystery I find bewildering. It is one thing to fathom why people land in one set of circumstances over another; it is quite another to understand why people respond so differently to their circumstances — for example, why some seem to elevate themselves above them while others are diminished by them. What the particular circumstances are seems to matter little. Some people make something of what they are given, however meager; others do nothing at all, or worse, squander what they have, though their inheritance is great. Why?

I have observed this mystery playing itself out in my work as a university professor. One student excels and another fails, though their abilities seem about the same. Background surely has some predictive value, but in my experience it falls short of providing a satisfying explanation. Human beings are more than the sum total of their background and experiences. They are free to determine their destiny, at least a little; but that little can amount to much over a lifetime.

A Lingering Question

We know that God redeems through Jesus Christ, completely and perfectly. We don't have to earn or accomplish our redemption as if it were a burden that rests on our shoulders alone. It is not a project but a gift, not something to achieve but something to receive. But a question still lingers. What can and should we expect from redemption? Will a Christian's story somehow read better than someone else's who doesn't believe in Christ's redemptive work? And what does "better" actually mean?

I am tempted at this point to provide an easy answer. Yes, I want to say, redemption promises a happy ending, a kind of return to the garden, where all is goodness and happiness and bliss. I want to assure you that redemption means your lot in life is bound to improve, your circumstances will become more favorable. I want to call your story redemptive if, after a painful divorce, you remarry again, this time successfully; or if, after months of unemployment, you land the ideal job; or if, after a period of sickness, your child recovers and ends up competing in the Olympics. But all of this assumes that favorable circumstances — remarriage, employment, health, success — capture the essence of redemption. Then the question becomes, Is a positive outcome really the point? Is happiness the proper goal? Is that what we can and should expect of God? It seems right, on the surface of things. Who doesn't desire a happy ending?

It would be nice indeed if redemption led to a good life, however we choose to define it. Patricia and I like to call it the ideal of the "gated community," which serves as a symbol of the good life for middle-class people — a big house in a safe neighborhood, a summer cottage, three successful children who live nearby, high-achieving grandchildren, a hobby or two, a group of good friends. Such a life promises a happy ending, and I for one like happy endings. I tend to read literature and watch films that end "redemptively," as I tell my kids, which is a code word in our house for a happy ending. In fact, they often say to me, "Dad, you better not see that film. It's too dark. There's no redemptive ending."

In truth, I don't actually believe in happy endings any more, at least not as they are traditionally defined. It was a peculiar detail in Genesis 3 that turned me in this new direction. The text says that after driving Adam and Eve out of the garden of Eden, God posted angelic guards at the entrance gate, forbidding reentry (Genesis 3:24). Thus God not only pushed Adam and Eve out of the garden, but he also refused to let them back in, which strikes me as odd, even mean. I can see officials at Disneyland expelling unruly students for a day. But never let them return? That seems unreasonable to me. After all, Disneyland is the happiest place on earth. Wouldn't you want unruly children to return? So why did God post the guards? Why deprive Adam and Eve of the blissful conditions of the garden? Didn't Adam and Eve need the security, perfection, and happiness of the garden even more *after* sinning against God?

I don't think so.

No More Garden

The worst thing to happen to us — sinful, selfish, and imperfect as we are — would be for us to live in a perfect world.

For at least two reasons: first, because over time we would make it imperfect anyway, which seems obvious enough; second, because we would begin to assume the world exists solely for the purpose of making us happy. But is happiness achieved by living in a perfect world? To my mind, happiness is less the product of an ideal environment and more the result of divine gift. Circumstances don't make us happy; only God can, enlarging our capacity to know and love him.

There are too many unhappy people who enjoy life's bounty and too many happy people who suffer from constant deprivation, which tells me that circumstances alone do not determine happiness. Why is it that Americans, whose circumstances are the envy of the world, tend to be less happy than people whose circumstances are far from envious? When Whitworth students return from study programs abroad, they invariably comment, "The people I met were so happy and generous, though they had virtually nothing! It made me feel ashamed."

In *The Last Battle*, C. S. Lewis describes the surprising response of a group of dwarves who end up in the Narnian version of Heaven. For some reason they are incapable of experiencing it. A banquet is set before them, but they think it filthy straw; light illumines the beauty of the country around them, but they see only darkness. What prevents them from realizing where they are? "The dwarves are for the dwarves," they keep saying. So nasty and selfish have they become that they have lost the capacity for happiness.

The perfection of the world is not enough. Something has to happen inside them.

What creates this capacity for genuine happiness? Ironically, it is the imperfection of the world—deprivation and suffering—that will do it, or better, will create the conditions for it. We need adversity, at least some of the time. It exposes our smallness, weakness, and selfishness; it reveals our need for God and enlarges our inward capacity for true happiness. Adversity does this work in the same way exercise grows muscle, by first breaking it down. Only people whose circumstances would appear to cause unhappiness can actually become truly happy. They stop requiring it from the world and learn to find it in God, the source of all that is good. Without adversity we would remain spoiled children who expect the world to conform to our every whim and wish.

It is easy to believe this truth when it remains an abstraction; it is another matter altogether when facing actual adversity. Abstract conviction and genuine belief do not always line up naturally and conveniently, especially in the wake of suffering. I can imagine what my response might have been if someone had asked me on September 26, 1991, "Do you believe that God works all things together for good?" or "Do you believe suffering really develops character and leads to hope?" I would have quickly and confidently replied, "Most certainly," to both questions. But at the time, I believed those promises more as theological abstraction than real conviction. My "most certainly" did in fact become far less certain and confident on September 28, 1991, for I faced a mess of pain and chaos that took time — a very long time — to understand and overcome.

In truth, I would have liked to remain a spoiled child. This option, however, was decisively and permanently eliminated on September 27, 1991. I struggled for many years before I could see any "good" come out of the accident, any character formed in me or in my children. I'm not even sure I wanted such good or such character. I rather preferred the life I had lost, and I longed to return to the familiar world and relationships of the past.

Over time, however, it became apparent to me that God indeed was at work in our lives. A new story began to emerge, however unclearly and slowly. It was a narrative that started in darkness but gave way ever so gradually to the dawn, and then finally emerged into the full light of day. The scene and setting had changed, to be sure. Much to my surprise, that change, as bad as it was, did not keep God from doing his redemptive work. If anything, God proved himself entirely capable of carrying on, using what appeared to be broken props and broken people. We simply had to give him the room to work and try our best to maintain faith when there didn't appear to be much reason to. Looking back some twenty years later, I can only express utter astonishment at what God has done. It makes me almost grateful for the loss itself, which I find incomprehensible.

Circumstances Play a Limited Role

It is this experience of God's redeeming work in my own life that leads me to believe, now more than ever, that circumstances play a limited role in the Christian life, providing little more than the context—scene and setting—for God's redemptive work. God uses adversity as well as prosperity to shape our lives: forming character in us, calling us to fruitful service, enabling us to love and trust him. I can say without a shadow of doubt that much good can come out of tragedy and suffering, as I have witnessed firsthand in the lives of so many, though the good resulting from tragedy does not justify the tragedy itself. In short, the event and the outcome are not the same thing. A good outcome never excuses or justifies a bad event.

But redemption is not about excuses or justifications. It's about God using both the "best" and the "worst" events to work out his redemptive plan. We see the quintessential example of the worst in the story of Jesus. I can't imagine anything more cruel and unjust than the crucifixion of the Son of God. It was an evil act perpetrated by ruthless and cowardly people. But God used that event to accomplish the salvation of the world. The act itself was bad, exceedingly bad; the outcome was good, good beyond measure. God made right what was profoundly, inexcusably wrong, and the result was the world's redemption.

Paul had this truth in mind when he wrote the final paragraph of Romans 8 (beginning with "And we know that in all things God works for the good ...").Well-meaning people often quote this passage at the most inopportune times, usually to comfort people who have recently experienced a loss, as if it is a kind of spiritual pain medication. However true the passage, it does not promise to medicate or eliminate sorrow. Paul did not write it to diminish the severity of suffering and the pain it causes. If anyone knew how bad suffering is, surely Paul was that person. On one occasion he even speaks of himself as being "under great pressure," to the point that he "despaired of life itself" (2 Corinthians 1:8). Paul was hardly a superficial triumphalist, an ancient version of the modern positive thinker.

Paul's point is that, however bad it may be, adversity has no power to thwart God's redemptive plan. No matter what our circumstances, God is good and works good. God will accomplish his purpose; he will redeem our lives. Jesus Christ provides the full guarantee. If God did not withhold such a gift, as perfect as it is, will he not give us everything else with him? Thus Paul writes:

> What, then, shall we say in response to these things? If God is for us, who can be against us? He who did not spare his own Son, but gave him up for us all—how will he not also, along with him, graciously give us all things? Who will bring any charge against those whom God has chosen? It is God who justifies.Who then is the one who condemns? No one. Christ Jesus who died—more than that, who was raised to life—is at the right hand of

God and is also interceding for us. Who shall separate us from the love of Christ? (Romans 8:31–35a)

That last question is rhetorical, of course. Paul simply could not conceive of any experience in this world that could separate us from God. He continues, "Shall trouble or hardship or persecution or famine or nakedness or danger or sword?" No, Paul says, God's power always conquers, not because of any inherent strength or greatness in us, weak and powerless as we are, but because of the infinite strength and greatness of God. Nothing, he says, "will be able to separate us from the love of God that is in Christ Jesus our Lord" (Romans 8:38–39). And he means exactly that—nothing.

Paul accepted life as it came to him or, as often seemed to be the case, as it came at him, and he did so robustly. He embraced—though he did not necessarily like—adversity (such as his mysterious "thorn in the flesh") because it reminded him of his weakness and drove him to God: "When I am weak, then I am strong" (2 Corinthians 12:10). Admitting his need, he turned toward God. It seems strange to us, of course, who think that the only adequate way to deal with adversity is to eliminate or overcome it. But Paul learned to thrive in it (2 Corinthians 4:7–14).

Not that Paul's life consisted of constant suffering. He experienced many moments of earthly—yes, earthly—happiness, too. He enjoyed friendships, success, honor, and influence. Strangely, it didn't seem to matter much either way. In short, he learned to be content, no matter what his circumstances, holding all things loosely. Both adversity and prosperity served the same purpose because his goal in life was not to avoid the one or to achieve the other. Here is how he described it:

> I am not saying this because I am in need, for I have learned to be content whatever the circumstances. I know what it is to be in need, and I know what it is to have plenty. I have learned the secret of being content in any and every situation, whether well fed or hungry, whether living in plenty or in want. I can do all this through him who gives me strength. (Philippians 4:11–13)

What mattered to Paul—the only thing that mattered to Paul—was life in Christ. Adversity and prosperity provided little more than scene and setting for the real story.

SPIRITUALLY AMBIDEXTROUS

This capacity to transcend circumstances was a central theme among a group of Christians who left their major mark in the third, fourth, and fifth centuries. The "Desert Fathers and Mothers," as they came to be called, emerged as a counter-cultural movement at a time when the church had started to enjoy the state's favor. Rejecting the corrosive influences of the culture, they chose to make the barren, lonely desert their base of operations. There they worshiped God, battled the devil, and practiced strict and austere spiritual disciplines (fasting, poverty, vigils, solitude, and the like). They wanted to become "spiritual athletes," thereby challenging the compromised faith that was slowly turning the church soft. They were odd and fanatical, to be sure; but they also demonstrated earnestness of faith and purpose.

These hermits, who were intent on living in seclusion, nevertheless attracted thousands of followers — so many, in fact, that one desert father observed that the desert had become a city. Many stayed in the desert for a lifetime; others visited for a few months or years and then left, spreading the movement elsewhere. One visitor, John Cassian, wrote two books about the hermits, distilling the wisdom of the great Egyptian masters of the movement.

One of those masters, Abba Theodore, used a peculiar word to describe disciples whose faith enabled them to transcend their circumstances. The word is *ambidextrous*, which, as you know, describes a person who is equally adept using either the right hand or left hand. In baseball, an ambidextrous person often functions as a switch-hitter. But Abba Theodore applied the term to spiritual matters. Ambidextrous disciples, he said, learn to live for Christ in both adversity and prosperity:

> This power we also can spiritually acquire, if by making a right and proper use of those things which are fortunate, and which seem to be "on the right hand," as well as those which are unfortunate and as we call it "on the left hand."[1]

Theodore noted how God uses both prosperity and

adversity to advance his purposes. Prosperity would seem to be preferable, of course, because it makes God seem good, the world seem right, and faith seem natural, as natural as writing with the dominant hand. Obviously, adversity does the opposite, making life hard for us. Temptation overruns us, doubt plagues us, routine bores us. Still, ambidextrous Christians, Cassian said, take both in stride, as Joseph, Ruth, and especially Jesus did; thus prosperity does not lead to carelessness, nor does adversity lead to despair. He wrote:

> We shall then be ambidextrous, when neither abundance nor want affects us, and when the former does not entice us to the luxury of a dangerous carelessness, while the latter does not draw us to despair, and complaining; but when, giving thanks to God in either case alike, we gain one and the same advantage out of good and bad fortune.[2]

God can use adversity as well as prosperity to enlarge our capacity to trust him and conform us to the image of his Son. They are tools in his hands, like the hammer and chisel Michelangelo used to sculpt his figures, setting them free from their marble prison. We don't need just the right circumstances to mature as Christians or to find happiness in life. For better or for worse, for richer or for poorer, in sickness and in health, God remains faithful and true. He uses whatever is at hand to make us his and make us like Christ. Again, circumstances play a limited role. They can play such a limited role because God never does. His entire being is devoted to our redemption. As Paul proclaimed so triumphantly, nothing can separate us from the love of God.

Personal Circumstances

I have reflected a great deal on the neutrality of circumstances over the past few years, and for a specific reason. After nineteen years of widowhood, I recently remarried. It was a weighty decision that required a great deal of reflection. My first wife, Lynda, and I married in 1971, during our college years. I was twenty-one and she was twenty-two. During the twenty years we were married, we lived in four states, had four children, earned three advanced degrees, served a church, and taught at two colleges. Marriage was a gift to us, though we had to work hard at it. We built a good life together and enjoyed great happiness with each other.

Then our family suffered the accident.

I can only describe the experience as a torrent of trauma, pain, and confusion that threatened to drown me. The needs of my three young children kept me afloat, for they clung to me as if I were a life raft. So I simply refused to go under. Over time, I settled into widowed life and slowly gained confidence that I could make it without Lynda as wife and mother. On occasion I thought about remarriage, viewing it primarily as a solution to a problem. After all, my kids did need a mother. But I could never quite shake the thought that what they needed most was not just any mother but their own mother, Lynda.

Single life became a spiritual discipline for me, a "state" in which to find contentment, as the apostle Paul put it. Was I ever lonely? Did I ever long for companionship? Was I ever exhausted by the responsibility? Did I ever worry about my kids? Yes, on all counts. But somehow life as a widower and single father became bearable and even meaningful. In short, I accepted the fact that we had become a family of four rather than six. Then the kids began to disappear, first to college and then to other places, some far away.

It was hard to let them go because I relished the life we shaped and shared together. The role I learned to play — a role I would not have chosen for myself — became familiar and comfortable to me, like a suit of clothes, at first appearing ugly and ill-fitting, that I slowly grew into and even came to like. Was I happy? I stopped thinking much about it, probably because I was too busy.

Then I met Patricia and fell hopelessly in love. Almost immediately I saw the problem. Not her, of course. She was — and is — wonderful. It was me. I felt torn. On the one hand, I was fiercely loyal to our family story, which seemed to be turning into a pretty good one. So why mess with it? On the other hand, I liked Patricia, and she liked me; we seemed a good match, too. So why end the relationship?

Our relationship grew under the watchful eye of friends. They warmed to the idea almost immediately, though they counseled us to proceed slowly. We were especially concerned about our children. We had heard too many stories about children who had suffered neglect through the process of a remarriage. We thought such a price was too high. But our children liked the idea of us, and they liked each other, too, especially because my two sons, David and John, and Patricia's two daughters, Morgan and Taylor, had known each other for many years. The time we shared together as two families showed us that remarriage might actually be good for all of us.

But I continued to feel unsettled. I had become so suspicious of "earthly happiness," as I liked to call it, that the very idea of it disturbed and unnerved me. I wondered if remarriage would make me a lesser Christian. In truth, I had become insufferably "spiritual," so much so that romantic love, one of God's good gifts, seemed like a compromise to me. Why Patricia chose to remain in the relationship is a testament to her patience and love, and to Morgan and Taylor's tolerance.

Eventually I discovered how self-righteous and foolish I was. I also learned that I was simply asking the wrong question. Did singleness or marriage really matter all that much? I knew that neither promised endless happiness or certain misery, that neither would make me a saint or a sinner. Which I chose seemed less important to me than why. Would I be willing to "get over myself," as a few friends strongly advised me to do, and embrace remarriage as a gift? Could I see that discipleship and happiness might actually be compatible?

Paul describes singleness and marriage as a "state," a set of circumstances that God can use to work redemption. The real action concerns what God has already done for us, how he is currently working in our lives, and how we respond. As Paul writes, whether slave or free, whether Jew or Gentile, whether married or single — in prosperity or adversity — only one thing matters. "I am saying this for your own good, not to restrict you, but that you may live in a right way in undivided devotion to the Lord" (1 Corinthians 7:35).

Patricia and I were married in August of 2010; it was a glorious wedding. Patricia's good friends, Terry and Kris, served as maid of honor; my sister and brother-in-law, Diane and Jack, as best man. A dear friend and colleague, Jim Edwards, performed the ceremony. Our children — my four (my son-in-law Jacob was included) and her two — surrounded us as witnesses. Patricia and I made vows to our children and friends first, and then to each other. The entire wedding party conferred a blessing on us, and the congregation confirmed it. We concluded the ceremony with communion. Thus did two stories merge into one.

The Divine Workshop

Marriage, like singleness, has become a form of spiritual discipline for me. Not that it has been laborious and odious. In the first six months we were married, I don't think I had ever laughed more, mostly at myself, as we made the necessary adjustments, such as learning how to share a home that both of us are by nature and experience inclined to run on our own terms, deciding how to manage money, and adapting to each other's rhythms.

Marriage requires hard work even under ideal conditions. It has an unrelenting quality to it. Day in, day out, a couple has to figure out how to do ordinary life together —divide chores, settle conflict, entertain guests, relate with children, and all the rest. No institution on earth forces you to learn the art of love quite like marriage. Biology might motivate you to love your children. Not so your spouse. What keeps a marriage going and growing is commitment —the daily discipline of love.

It is a great accomplishment to learn how to love another human being well, and marriage affords a grand opportunity for just that. Marriage is one of God's workshops; he uses it as a tool to change our lives. It doesn't ensure happiness, of course—I warn couples to purge that expectation before they make vows at the altar; but marriage can develop and deepen our capacity for happiness. For that matter, so can singleness. In fact, most kinds of circumstances can do that, for God doesn't seem all that selective. The entire world is his; it is all part of his divine workshop.

No doubt your circumstances are different from mine. You might be single, as I was, and long for marriage, or married and wish you were single. You might be unemployed, eager to take whatever job comes your way, or employed but ready to quit. You might love everything about your life and hope to keep it exactly as it is for as long as you can, or you might despise everything about your life and want to change it completely. Sometimes such a change is possible and reasonable, too. Still, it is too easy and convenient to assume that a change of circumstances will solve all problems — some, perhaps, but certainly not all, for no matter how much you change, you will always be stuck with yourself. Whether you get married and find a job, stay married and at your job, or get out of a marriage and quit a job, you cannot get rid of the self you are. And God is intensely interested in that self. He will use whatever state you are in to transform your life.

RIGHT WHERE YOU ARE

The apostle Paul is clear about the relative insignificance of our circumstances. In fact, he states that a preoccupation with circumstances — such as circumcision or uncircumcision — can keep us from being attentive to God's ultimate will for our lives, which is to live a life of faith and obedience right where we are:

> Was a man already circumcised when he was called? He should not become uncircumcised. Was a man uncircumcised when he was called? He should not be circumcised. Circumcision is nothing and uncircumcision is nothing. Keeping God's commands is what counts. Each person should remain in the situation they were in when God called them. (1 Corinthians 7:18–20)

If anyone knew about the vicissitudes of circumstances, surely it was John Calvin, the sixteenth-century preacher and reformer of Geneva, who enjoyed a short but happy marriage and great success in ministry but who also faced fierce opposition through most of his adult life. He experienced both prosperity and adversity, and God used both to advance his redemptive work. Calvin believed that earthly prosperity is a divine gift, which we can enjoy in good conscience, assuming we do so as God intended. But he also recognized that prosperity is fleeting. Sooner or later we will discover that adversity is an inescapable reality, for we live in a fallen world. In short, it is impossible to have one without the other.

But it is possible — and right — to live for and love God *in* both. On the one hand, Calvin wrote, we should thank God for prosperity but exercise moderation in how we enjoy it, lest we become idolatrous: "For many so enslave all their senses to delights that the mind lies overwhelmed. Many are so delighted with marble, gold, and pictures that they become marble, they turn, as it were, into metals and are like painted figures."[3]

On the other hand, he wrote that we should look to God for perspective, strength, and comfort when facing adversity, which, even under the best of circumstances, is bound to afflict us: "How necessary this disposition will appear if you weigh the many chance happenings to which we are subject."[4] God is still God, writing his redemptive story. In the end, all will be well. Not that we should dismiss or ignore the severity of the pain we feel in the face of adversity. Calvin affirmed the legitimacy of human emotion. Still, however real, emotions do not define reality. God defines reality, and that reality is redemptive.

I am not suggesting that we pursue adversity as if it were inherently virtuous. We might follow a course of life that leads to adversity, but never for the sake of adversity itself, which would be masochistic. There is nothing particularly good or pleasant about adversity, and God does not ask us to call it good or to like it but to believe that he can and will work good out of it. He invites us to submit, not to the adversity itself but to him *in* our adversity.

I am not suggesting we reject prosperity either, as if it were inherently evil. Prosperity, after all, is God's gift, as Calvin pointed out. But it poses certain risks all the same, for it can foster a spirit of entitlement, selfishness, and complacency. That all is well in our little world does not mean that all is well in the wider world, God's world (a subject to which we will return in chapter 10). Thus prosperity has its problems, too. After all, who needs God if life is good? Again, there are no guarantees. As I have already argued, circumstances play a limited role, providing scene and setting for God's redemptive work. Their ultimate impact depends on how we respond to God in and through them.

I tend to be ruthlessly realistic about life. Like anyone, of course, I want my life to turn out well, which it has, at least for the most part, and thankfully so. But the occasions in which it hasn't have been profoundly disruptive, and they have forced me to my knees, reminding me how little control I really have. I have taken my hits, as most people do. But there is more to it than that, for I have also experienced the redemption that has come out of those hits.

Perhaps you have, too. The letters and emails I have received over the years and the many conversations I have had about suffering remind me that people can be — and often are — enlarged through their suffering, becoming extraordinary individuals, full of wisdom, goodness, and love. They have come to know God deeply, forgiven perpetrators, adopted special-needs children after losing children, accepted sickness with grace, devoted themselves to noble causes, and so much more. I have seen the results of the experience of adversity in countless others, and I like what I see. The image of that weathered tree comes to mind once again.

Life Simply Is

It might sound simplistic, but circumstances really do seem to play a limited role, whatever our lot in life happens to be — tragedy and happiness, singleness and marriage, riches and poverty, sickness and health. I might prefer one above the other, as I'm sure you would as well, and rightly so; I might even get to choose one above the other. But my power of choice is limited, and so is yours. Sooner or later we will face surprises along the way — some a delight, others a horror.

Life as we know and experience it from day to day and from season to season simply is, whether we like it or not. We enjoy prosperity for a time, perhaps a long time; then we face adversity. Of course natural preference will always lean in the direction of prosperity. Who doesn't want the good life? But natural preference will not always prevail.

No doubt there are also reasons why life takes on the particular shape it does. We would be wise, I think, to explore what those reasons are, and we might learn a great deal that will help us, especially if we keep making the same mistakes and falling into the same traps. After the accident, I certainly benefited from regular visits to a counselor, dear Rachel, who challenged me to explore all kinds of issues having to do with family of origin, loss, marriage, and parenthood. Her probing questions and useful advice enabled me to turn the accident into an opportunity to take on issues that would have otherwise been conveniently — and foolishly — ignored. We covered a lot of ground during those sessions. At first it only exacerbated the pain of the loss; in the long run, it ended up playing a major role in the redemption of our family.

But all the counseling in the world, however helpful, did not and could not erase one undeniable fact — the accident happened and people died. As much as I learned from Rachel, I never did figure out how to recover and reclaim my old life, which was lost in a tangle of metal on a lonely highway in rural Idaho.

Then I faced — as all of us must face somewhere along the way — that lingering question I mentioned earlier in the chapter: *What can and should I expect from redemption?* Our natural inclination is to desire, expect, and probably even demand the life of the garden — some ideal we imagine in our head and perhaps experienced for a time in real life. We want life to be just so, to return to a version of the garden that appeals to our immediate interests. But God has closed and locked the gate to the garden, blocking the way. The days of the garden are over, and, as we well know, they have been for a long time.

But all is not lost. God is cultivating a different kind of garden; and that garden is you and me — the relationship we have with God, the persons we are becoming, the life we live, the good we accomplish. Surely Paul had something like that in mind when he described Christians as emitting the "aroma of Christ," the fragrance of the garden (2 Corinthians 2:15). What he implies is that God is making *us* into his garden. He intends to use the beauty, aroma, and fruitfulness of our lives as a sign of and witness to his redemptive work in the world.

CHAPTER 5

Plot

Plot provides the connection point between two things: story on the one hand (chapter 3), scene and setting on the other (chapter 4). *Story* provides a narrative structure, some kind of movement that leads from past to present to future. Life is never static, not even when it seems to be. It is always going somewhere. Nor is life random, a series of disconnected events, like a deck of cards tossed into the air. Contrary to how it might seem, the story of your life has meaning, purpose, and momentum to it. Likewise, *scene and setting* are like the props, background, and backdrop on a stage. It is the stuff of one's inheritance, like racial and ethnic origin, family background, facial features, body type, talents, opportunities, prosperity, and adversity — in short, the circumstances of life.

Plot embodies the narrative thread that grows out of scene and setting, establishing a specific course for the story of our lives. It is always particular, idiosyncratic, and unique to each of us. It is a little like the process of theatrical improvisation. An actor has to rely on wits and experience to act out a story on the spur of the moment, using resources close at hand. An audience member shouts out a story line: "You're walking in Central Park, and you run into an old friend you haven't seen for thirty years." Another person hands him a random set of props—umbrella, gloves, whistle, guitar. The actor's job is to act out a story with a specific plot, invented on the spot, using the props he has been given.

As in the case of improvisation, so in the case of real life: you don't have complete control over your life. Things get tossed at you, and you must figure out what to do with it all. You have been born into circumstances beyond your control, inherited opportunities and problems passed on through gene pool and family background and life experiences, and faced losses you did not choose. What can you do with what you have been given?

MOVES ON THE CHESSBOARD

Chess players will tell you that every move on a chessboard, except the first, is subject to one major limitation —all previous moves, which determine the configuration of the chessboard at any given moment. Chess players know before a match begins that the progression of the match is bound to depart from their original plan, but they don't quit just because the match proceeds in an unanticipated direction. Only children would do that. The skill and art of the chess player is to make the best possible move based on the opponent's previous move. This "given" on the chessboard puts the player in either an advantageous or perilous position. It does little good to wish the board were configured differently, wasting time and energy fantasizing something that does not exist. The board *as it is* creates the conditions for the next move, which almost always include more than one option up until the final "checkmate."

A similar dynamic is at work in our lives. Life as it comes to us and at us creates the conditions for our next move—and there are almost always multiple ways we can respond. In fact, the quest for complete control over our circumstances might actually sabotage our ability to make good decisions, for it inclines us to think there is only one way—our way—to realize them.

Take the ideal "future" someone has in mind. A young woman assumes she will marry and have children. She imagines a quiet home filled with happy, creative, and obedient children, all serious students and artists. Meanwhile, her husband-to-be imagines a house full of noise, play, and friends, with his children involved in competitive athletics. Neither, of course, will get exactly what he or she wants. The same could be said of a couple who imagines the ideal wedding and honeymoon, a woman who envisions landing the ideal job, a man who fantasizes building the ideal house, the teenager who dreams about attending the ideal college. In each case something will occur to alter their plans, most likely disappointing them. What will they choose then?

Such is the crisis I faced when our family of six suddenly became a family of four. It was a delicate business to honor the past but lean into the future, to remember the old but embrace the new, however unwanted it was. I remember making one little decision—at least it seemed that way at the time—that took on greater significance as the years passed.

I decided to spend an entire Thanksgiving break at home and to invite an eclectic group of people over for Thanksgiving dinner. Still very young, my kids nevertheless worked with me in the kitchen. I'm not sure the food was very good. I still have a hard time getting the turkey done at the right time, as my family will tell you. But it was an attempt to challenge the assumption—as much ours as anyone else's—that our family embodied some special case of neediness. Now we are veterans of hosting dozens of such feasts, having invited hundreds into our home for Thanksgiving, Christmas, and Easter. The food has gotten better, too. If anything, my children have surpassed me as chefs, which I suppose isn't saying much, each having developed their own signature dishes.

You would find another symbol of the significance of our family story if you visited us during Christmas. This past Christmas we had twelve homemade stockings hanging from the mantel. Two represent the sacredness of people who left the family story prematurely—Lynda's and Diana Jane's. Four represent the continuation of the story—Catherine's, David's, John's, and mine. Six represent the surprising twists in the story that have occurred over the past few years—Patricia's, Morgan's, Taylor's, Jacob's, Kelli's, and Annalise's. Soon a stocking for a grandson will adorn the mantel, probably hanging right in the middle. Old and new are all mingled together—symbols of a plot that has turned in a strange and wonderful direction, welcoming new friends to our Thanksgiving table and adding new Christmas stockings to the mantel.

Your circumstances are different from mine, and they are probably no better or no worse than mine either. How often do people get to live out a story that conforms to their preconceived ideal, unfolds according to their plan, and takes place within a scene and setting of their design? I know a few such cases, but not many. Most of us step into a story and inherit a set of circumstances that falls short of the ideal, sometimes far short. Still, we do have the power to determine trajectory, shape the plot, and set a course. I will not diminish the difficulty of the task; neither can I deny the drama and adventure and thrill of it all. I am sure that all of us know many people who, facing severe problems, have lived out stories that have become meaningful beyond measure. More often than not, they made things up as they went along. Like seasoned actors, they improvised. But by the grace of God and through the guidance of the Holy Spirit, all turned out well — exceedingly well.

Inside the Story

When reading a story, we stand outside the time sequence of the narrative as the plot progresses. If we wish, we can read the last chapter first to discover how it ends even before we learn how it begins. We don't have the same luxury in the case of our own story. The reason is simple enough — we are in the middle of it. We bear the imprint of the past, with no power to change it; we look to the future, with no power to control it. We are confined to the present, whether ideal or miserable.

We might pass through periods in which the plot is clear, compelling, and obvious to us, as if standing atop a mountain peak on a cloudless day, where we can see the past and future stretch out for miles behind or before us and thus view everything in proper proportion and perspective, every experience and relationship with absolute clarity. We see the whole of life in one glorious glance. It will seem like a beautiful dream to us, even when viewing experiences that we remember as being especially difficult and painful. We will be able to think this way because we stand above it all.

But as we all know, such a transcendent perspective is fleeting. We will eventually have to leave the mountain peak and descend once more into the valley below, returning to the wild and rugged terrain of normal life. What seemed easy from atop the mountain peak will become hard again; what made sense will confuse and bewilder us; what was filled with light will turn into darkness.

Trappist monk and author Thomas Merton warned that sooner or later every one of us will have to descend into the abyss and enter the darkness. Schooled in the mystical tradition, he was especially attracted to the writings of John of the Cross, who taught that passing through the "dark night of the senses" and the "dark night of the soul" is both inevitable and necessary in the life of faith. It is the only way to be weaned from all earthly attachments, even religious, to mature in faith, and to surrender our cherished — and imagined — control. It is a simple and easy task to live by faith when light shines all around us and God provides ample evidence of his presence, goodness, and power. Then again, faith always comes easily when it isn't really needed, as love comes easily in romance. But such easy faith must come to an end in order to become true faith, as romantic love eventually must include the disciplined work of marital love. We must leave the mountain, where all seems clear, and descend into the terrifying darkness below.

At this point, Merton argues, our own efforts are entirely useless. Faith is not faith when it sees, wills, and gets what it wants; it is not the same as self-confidence, natural optimism, or positive thinking. Merton is especially critical of "holy people," as he calls them, who always seem to be in the know and in control. Their natural confidence, which they confuse with genuine faith, is bound to come to an end. It *must* come to an end, for it is in fact the opposite of faith. "As soon as they reach the point where they can no longer see the way and guide themselves by their own light, they refuse to go any further. They have no confidence in anyone except themselves. Their faith is largely an emotional illusion."[5]

We might on occasion ascend to a mountain peak and enjoy the view. But we cannot and should not stay there for long, not if we want our story to continue in a redemptive direction, for a meaningful plot always pushes us forward, and eventually downward. It requires descent into the darkness. Merton affirms that faith is only faith when it depends on God, not on the self:

> But when the time comes to enter the darkness in which we are naked and helpless and alone; in which we see the insufficiency of our greatest strength and the hollowness of our strongest virtues; in which we have nothing of our own to rely on; and nothing in our nature to support us, and nothing in the world to guide us or give us light—then we find out whether or not we live by faith.[6]

I honestly wish there were another way. I wish I could assure you that the story of your life will unfold as conveniently and happily as the plot of a predictable (and boring) novel. But predictability is not always good, control not always preferable, happiness not always the ideal. No one likes to read a boring story or to live a boring life. As we know, being inside a story is a very different experience from rising above it, living a story very different from reading it. We have no choice but to let the mystery of it unfold, which requires faith; we choose to believe God is working redemption when nothing assures us that he is. Even if it is as tiny as a mustard seed, such faith will affect the choices that set a trajectory and shape the plot.

SIX MAPS

We can't step out of our own story to read it as if it were a novel, for the obvious reason that we are *in* the story, living it out chapter by chapter. But we can become familiar with the plots of other's stories, which will help us understand our own better. Such familiarity is a little like viewing a topographical map of a mountain range.

A map, of course, is not the actual landscape; it cannot substitute for being there. My kids would not have been pleased had I suggested we study maps of national parks rather than visit them. Still, when we did explore the parks, we found it helpful to consult a map. That way we could observe the contours of the landscape, see where we had come from and where we were going, identify major sites along the way (such as lakes and mountain peaks), and avoid getting lost. A map couldn't answer all our questions or solve all our problems—change bad weather, for example, make the trail level and smooth, or get us to a destination faster—but it was still exceedingly useful. Even when our sight was limited, conditions miserable, terrain difficult, and the trail obscure, we always knew where we were.

The biblical story is like a map. Like any good map, it shows the broad landscape of God's redemptive plan and the myriad of details that make it interesting and inviting. There is the grand narrative—creation, fall, redemption; and the little plots and subplots that contribute to the narrative, as we saw in the case of the story of Ruth. No two plots are ever alike. But there are certainly some common themes or maps. I want to take a closer look at six of these common plot maps in the biblical story in the hope that one of them might help you to make sense of your life story. As we learn from many biblical stories, we have the power to choose, and the choices we make really matter.

Map 1: Passing on a New Legacy

Perhaps you come from a bankrupt family background, which has left in its wake nothing but betrayal and pain and loss. Your father is an alcoholic, your stepmother demanding and bitter. Your sister is already on her second marriage and your brother has been in and out of drug rehab for a decade. You flunked out of college twice before pushing your way through, and you struggle with depression.

About five years ago a coworker befriended you. You were suspicious at first because he identified himself as a Christian, but over time you became good friends. He eventually invited you to an Easter service at his church. The pastor's message captured your interest, and the people you met seemed happy, warm, and authentic. You started to attend worship more often until you were a regular. Then you became a Christian, which came as a surprise to you considering how dismissive you had been of Christianity. Shortly after your conversion an older couple invited you to join a Bible study; they have since become like parents to you.

You soon discover, however, that conversion to Christ does not erase the past or allow you to escape its consequences. Your background is still a mess, a heavy anchor you drag behind you. What can—what should—you do? One option, in my mind the redemptive one, is to face the past squarely and live out a story that sets a different and better trajectory. Instead of passing it on in that same messy condition to the next generation, you pass it on as a positive legacy. In short, you turn a deficit into a surplus; inheriting a mess, you bequeath a blessing.

I have a concrete example in mind. Gregg stumbled into our family circle many years ago after he started to attend Whitworth University, where I teach. Both of his biological parents have each been married five times, a reflection of the chaos in which he grew up. Living on his own by the age of sixteen, he rented a small apartment, worked at a McDonald's to make money, and finished high school. He also started using drugs. How he ended up at a Christian university like Whitworth is a mystery to me. However it happened, he became a Christian at Whitworth, found a group of strong Christian friends (still his best friends), and attached himself to several Christian families, including ours.

After graduation, he worked in a youth position for a few years and then attended Princeton Seminary. He met and married Kim while serving a church in Charlotte, North Carolina. By then he sensed a call to become an army chaplain. His career choice is a reflection of the legacy he wants to leave to the next generation, transforming the disease of his past into a healing antidote for others. "The military attracts lots of young men who come from my kind of background," Gregg explains. "They are rootless and lost and undisciplined. These are just the people I understand and can serve best."

Gregg spent a year in Afghanistan, where he worked

fourteen-hour days offering pastoral care to soldiers facing every problem imaginable — including the problems Gregg himself had faced while growing up. Now serving in a church again, Gregg continues to follow the same trajectory. He has done the hard work of converting the deficit of the past into a surplus for future generations. As I recently learned, he will soon be able to pass that legacy on to a child.

The story of King Josiah provides a worthy biblical example of this same plot theme. His father and grandfather, Amon and Manasseh, were two of Judah's worst kings; they worshiped foreign deities, shed innocent blood, and even sacrificed their children to foreign gods. So corrupt was Manasseh, in fact, that he led the people astray, "so that they did more evil than the nations the LORD had destroyed before the Israelites" (2 Kings 21:9).

How, then, do we explain the godly reign of Josiah? His story seems an anomaly, for nothing in his immediate background accounts for the drastic redirection of plot that occurred during his reign as king. He rediscovered "the Book of the Law," which had been stuffed into some temple storage room and forgotten, and he reinstated its laws and rituals, including the observance of Passover (2 Kings 22–23). He repented for the sins of his fathers, suppressed the practice of idolatry, mandated that religious officials do their work with integrity, and honored the prophets who proclaimed God's word. "Neither before nor after Josiah was there a king like him who turned to the LORD as he did—with all his heart and with all his soul and with all his strength, in accordance with all the Law of Moses" (2 Kings 23:25). Inheriting a legacy of evil, he passed on a legacy of righteousness and goodness. He became what we might call a "transitional" generation.

It is true that the sins of the fathers are often passed on to the third and fourth generations. One generation of alcoholism, unfaithfulness, pornography, drug addiction, greed, ambition, insecurity, adultery, abuse, laziness, injustice, and bitterness hands off the problem and pain to the next, which does the same yet again, thus perpetuating an endless cycle of destruction. But one courageous person can set a trajectory of redemption to reverse that cycle, as did both Gregg and Josiah, turning bankruptcy into spiritual riches.

Is God calling you to transform the brokenness of your past into a legacy of blessing to the next generation? Could that be the plot of your story?

Map 2: Stewarding a Bounty of Resources

This second plotline is similar to the first, but with one notable exception. Rather than inheriting a spiritual deficit, you inherit a surplus of resources and choose to develop and ultimately invest those resources in God's kingdom work. Perhaps your mother has a reputation for being the best physician in town, your father for being a "good Samaritan" because he has helped so many people through his network of business contacts and through his financial generosity. Your pastor has been at the church for twenty-nine years, and the congregation loves this faithful shepherd now more than ever. Your home serves as a gathering place for a large circle of friends. You are a great athlete and competent musician, and you played the lead role in the senior class play. You attended a prestigious college and graduate school. You get the idea: success comes as easily and naturally to you as swimming to a fish or flying to a bird.

What now? You can compromise the values that helped to amass this bountiful inheritance; you can hoard or spend it as if it belongs to you alone; you can squander it until there is little or nothing left, as the prodigal son did. The Bible tells several cautionary tales of such failures, and none is more sobering than the story of King Solomon. He inherited a stable kingdom, great wealth, a legacy of faith, and opportunity to build on what his father, King David, had left him. He started well. But then he became intoxicated by his own power, married recklessly, compromised faith, and enslaved his own people. After his death, the kingdom of Israel split in two, a breach that never healed. He inherited a fortune, but he passed on a pittance.

Then again, history also tells encouraging stories. Susannah Wesley gave birth to nineteen children, ten of whom survived to adulthood. She taught them to read and write, spent time alone with each one, and nurtured them in the Christian faith. Two of them, John and Charles, became the leaders of the Methodist movement, which was instrumental in the conversion of countless people in eighteenth-century England.

Contemporaries of the Wesley brothers, Jonathan and Sarah Edwards had ten children, all of whom survived to adulthood. Like Susannah Wesley, they loved those children well and challenged them to become followers of Jesus. Their influence produced generations of godly leaders in American history, including platoons of statesmen, ministers, and missionaries. In both cases, the investment of parents in their children had a profound impact on the generations that followed, largely because those children, the beneficiaries of a rich heritage, chose stewardship over selfishness. We are still benefitting from the tradition of faith and service that was passed on through these generations.

Is God calling you to invest your abundant resources in future generations? Could that be the plot of your story?

Map 3: Pursuing a Noble Vision

Vision usually emerges out of the interaction of two basic forces—life experience on the one hand, and a sense of calling on the other. Sometimes only one experience, which hardly seemed significant at the time of its occurrence, can function as the catalyst for one's life work. A bad teacher in junior high inspires you to start a charter school; the loss of a friend to an overdose leads you to found a rehab center; a church conflict pushes you into the ministry; a broken leg causes you to consider a career as an orthopedic surgeon. Germinating over time, like new plants after a long winter, a vision begins to take shape. You get the training you need, develop a strategy, assemble a team of people, marshal and manage resources, press on through failure, and eventually accomplish the vision.

Surely one of the greatest visionaries in world history is the apostle Paul, who recruited, organized, trained, and deployed dozens of young leaders to evangelize and plant churches throughout the Roman world. Ephesus, a city of some 250,000, became his center of operations for three years. Pagan religions were ubiquitous in his day; temples, shrines, monuments, and statues of emperors and gods dominated urban landscapes like Ephesus (still apparent today when observing the excavated ruins). Paul did not leave behind much material evidence of his ministry. But he did leave behind changed lives, living stones rather than lifeless temples and monuments. He was so effective, in fact, that pagan merchants and craftsmen in Ephesus instigated a riot to protest his influence. Their profits took a nosedive when a significant minority of the population converted to Christ and no longer bought pagan religious merchandise or visited the temple of Artemis (Acts 19). By the time Paul left the stage of history, both gospel and church were well established in the Roman world.

It is easy to cite as examples those few people throughout history who have achieved unusual success — church planters like the apostle Paul, missionaries like Hudson Taylor and Mary Slessor, and social reformers like William Wilberforce and Martin Luther King Jr. Most books and sermons do exactly that, which has the effect of intimidating and discouraging ordinary people like you and me. *I could never have that kind of impact*, we say to ourselves. *I could never accomplish such feats.* These figures did accomplish great things for God's kingdom, as we well know. But noble visions do not have to be so grandiose or the results so far reaching. Most of us do our work at the local level; our reach will be smaller in scope, but perhaps deeper.

In the past decade two Whitworth graduates chose to stay in Spokane and launch Christian nonprofits to meet practical needs in the community. Mark founded Cup of Cool Water to reach homeless teenagers, and Brent started Global Neighborhood to help refugees adjust to life in America. Over the years they have enlisted, trained, and deployed hundreds of volunteers, raised hundreds of thousands of dollars, and invested themselves in people whom the rest of us tend to overlook. Neither of these former students is getting rich; neither is becoming famous. Still, they are pursuing a noble vision and doing good work for the kingdom.

Is God calling you to accomplish some vision, great or small, for his kingdom? Could that be the plot of your story?

Map 4: Bearing a Heavy Burden

God calls some people to take on a hard task and shoulder a heavy burden. The story of Esther explores just that theme. Only one person was in a position to intervene. Haman hated Mordecai and his race of people, the Jews; he wanted to exterminate them all, and he plotted a scheme to do it. Made aware of the danger, Mordecai exhorted the new queen, his young cousin Esther, to appeal to the king. Accountable to no one, the king could do as he pleased; he was under no obligation even to give the queen an audience, to say nothing about responding to her request. But Mordecai persisted. He told Esther that God would act somehow to save the Jews, if not through her then through someone else. Still, she was their best hope: "Who knows but that you have come to your royal position for such a time as this?" (Esther 4:14).

The prophet Jeremiah, sometimes referred to as the weeping prophet, lived out a similar plotline, except in his case he met with failure rather than success—or so it would seem. God commanded him to warn and rebuke kings, priests, and people during a period of intense national suffering. The people resented Jeremiah because they wanted to hear a hopeful word. Who could blame them? Instead, Jeremiah's message was unrelentingly harsh. He never aspired to be a prophet in the first place, and he suffered horribly during the many years of his public ministry. In the end, he witnessed the destruction of Jerusalem. No one would choose to live this kind of story or follow such a plot. It has to be chosen for us. It is therefore highly individual and idiosyncratic, subject to what seems to be providential calling more than personal desire and ambition.

The character of Frodo in J. R. R. Tolkien's Lord of the Rings trilogy fits that description perfectly. As a hobbit, Frodo loved the pastoral life of the Shire, where he could eat six meals a day, drink beer, keep a garden, read a good book, smoke his pipe, chat with friends, and enjoy plenty of leisure. He had no ambition to be a great man and accomplish great deeds; he only wanted to live a quiet and peaceable life.

Ironically, it was those very qualities that suited him for the mission he—and only he—could fulfill, which was to carry the evil Ring of Power to Mount Doom, where it could be destroyed.

Like Esther, Jeremiah, and Frodo, some people are uniquely called to do a special work for God, a work requiring resourcefulness and fortitude. Sometimes it comes down to just one person, who happens to be in the right place at the right time. Only someone like Abraham Lincoln, president of a divided country, was in a position to fight for the abolition of slavery and the preservation of the union. Only someone like Dietrich Bonhoeffer, a child of privilege and educated in the best German institutions of his day, was in a position to lead the Confessing Church Movement and train pastors in an illegal underground seminary during the Nazi regime. Only someone like Martin Luther King Jr., trained in classical rhetoric and theology, called into ministry, and committed to nonviolent protest, was in a position to lead the civil rights movement. Still, Lincoln, Bonhoeffer, and King, however gifted, had to accept the heavy burden assigned to them, which led to considerable conflict, suffering, and early death.

Some people are assigned a heavy burden in life, and only they are in a position to bear it. Only they can love a disabled child, lead the fight for a just but unpopular cause, nurse a declining and divided church back to health, or reconcile estranged friends. And only God can issue the call and supply the power to fulfill it. For who would ever choose to bear this kind of burden? Who would be capable of it?

Is God calling you to bear such a burden? Could that be the plot of your story?

Map 5: Triumph through Suffering

Our family absorbed a significant blow some twenty years ago when three generations of women — my mother, my wife, and my daughter — died in an accident. What seems plain to me now, however, is that the accident was more like an interruption to our family story rather than a defining symbol of that story. In truth, our story was (before the accident) and continued to be (after the accident) fairly good, normal, and happy. The suffering we endured was the exception, not the rule.

Other stories do not unfold so nicely. Some people seem to suffer for a lifetime, experiencing one loss after another, like a cancer that continues to spread in spite of the extreme measures we take to defeat it. They face a myriad of health problems, their spouses keep losing jobs or money, their children become wayward, their best friends fall into sin or move away. It is a mystery to me why some people suffer so much and others so little.

When stories do not seem to turn out very well, it is natural — and right — to hope and pray for change. But what if our prayers to alter the plot go unanswered, our efforts to stop the bleeding fail, and the suffering continues? What do we do then? We choose to believe that God is still God, working redemption—if not in our circumstances, then certainly in us. Sometimes what happens in people is more significant than what happens to them or for them; sometimes who they become is more important than what they overcome or accomplish.

Inner transformation could be—and often is—the real plot of the redemptive story, which is summed up in God's power made perfect in human weakness. Circumstances that would logically lead to self-pity, bitterness, and despair, instead produce gratitude, holiness, and joy. I think of those weathered trees in Banff National Park. The conditions under which they live are hardly hospitable, exposed as they are to such harsh weather. They bear no fruit as, say, an apple tree does, which would not be able to survive in such a climate for one season. But there is fruit on those trees all the same, the fruit of character, for they have strength, resilience, and beauty.

I have long been both intrigued and terrified by the story of Job. You know how it unfolds. Job is a good man—so good, in fact, that God himself praises Job as an example of faith and generosity. But an adversary in the heavenly court, Satan, suggests that Job is a man of such faith and goodness because he is rewarded for it. Take away the reward, Satan says to God, and Job will spit in his face. So God allows Satan to put Job to the test. Job loses everything: his children, his wealth and health, his reputation. Utterly destitute, Job sits in silence and laments his faith. He has no idea why he has suffered so severely. He cries, questions, and disputes; but he refuses to curse God. Of course, he has no idea of what is happening in the court of Heaven; he does not know that a great cloud of witnesses is watching breathlessly to see if he will continue to believe in God when there is no apparent reason for it. Job's life is suffering; but there is more to it than that. His redemption consists, at least in part, in the intimacy he experiences with God and the faithful and true man he becomes.

Is God calling you to triumph through your suffering? Could that be the plot of your story?

Map 6: Honoring the Ordinary

Some stories don't seem to have much of a plot at all, at least not anything with much drama to it. Some people simply live an ordinary life; perhaps this is true for you. You come from a good family and you live a decent life. Your kids are grown and gone; you own a comfortable house —nothing fancy of course—and you drive an old, reliable minivan, which you used to tote your kids around for fifteen years. You teach in a middle school and have attended the same church for more years than you would care to count. No one has ever bothered to ask you to share your testimony, for they don't think there is really much of a story to tell.

Could the plot of your story be something as simple, elegant, and significant as the ordinary life you lead, which you turn into a kind of art form? You wake up every morning grateful for the day; you volunteer for mundane jobs without fanfare and perform daily tasks with joy and integrity. You care for people without drawing much attention to yourself, welcome them into your home, do their yard work when they're not able to, make them food when they're sick, baby-sit their kids when they're in a pinch, and offer financial support when they ask. You grow a garden and write notes of encouragement and make nice things for people. And you take time every day to pray for people in need, interceding for those who are too distraught to pray for themselves.

I know many people who live just this kind of life, even in my own neighborhood. One family takes care of several widows who live on the block, another has two Saudi students living with them, and still another invites people over for dinner several times a week, though they rarely receive dinner invitations from others. The Pulitzer Prize winning novel *Gilead* consists of a long, reflective letter written by a terminally ill father to his young son, who the father hopes will read and appreciate it when he gets older. Moving along at a leisurely pace, the letter contains little drama or tragedy. It is rich instead in ordinariness, and it bears witness to a life lived well because it is lived every day for God. Such is the power of redemption; it transforms even the routines of life into something holy, like turning the common elements of water, bread, and wine into means of grace.

Is God calling you to live your ordinary life for Jesus, turning it into a kind of art form? Could that be the plot of your story?

These six maps are not exhaustive, of course. There are others, I am sure. They provide a sample of various plots, already lived out in the stories of others who have gone before us, that will help us understand our own. I have observed the usefulness of studying these maps in myself, and also in my kids. This past week my son David asked me to proofread and comment on a job application he is sending to a search committee. I read his cover letter, resume, and essays. One of those essays caught my attention. Asked to reflect on his "spiritual journey," he stated that he did not come to faith in a moment of time but grew into it over time. *That* he believes is more important to him, he wrote, than when or how he first believed. Besides, he said, faith itself is a gift of God's grace. He reflected on the accident as well. He wrote that he could no more explain why such a horrible tragedy occurred than he could explain why his life has been so good since it occurred.

There it is, I thought to myself: *story.*

There it is for all of us. We are living out a redemptive story, redemptive because God is in it. Assuming God is in your story, how can you read the landscape of your life right now? What kind of plot is unfolding? What is the narrative thread? And what kind of trajectory should you set at this stage of life? These are the right questions to ask. Not that answers will come easily, if at all. It is always easier to ask questions than to answer them. But sometimes asking the right question is all we need to get us moving. Who knows what will happen then?

Author

It is time now to meet the author of the redemptive story. I am referring, of course, to God. It might seem an odd choice to have waited until chapter 6 to be introduced to the author. God is, after all, *the* author, which means he occupies the place of supremacy and stands above the story as its creator. So why did I wait so long to introduce him? Because in most cases we're only interested in learning more about an author after we have started reading his or her stories. If the stories capture, move, and intrigue us, then we become increasingly curious about the one who wrote them.

I read several of C. S. Lewis's books before I read anything about Lewis; I studied the writings of Dietrich Bonhoeffer before I studied the man himself. It was the brilliance of their writing that drove me to learn more about the authors. In each case, I asked, "Who is this man who could write with such genius?" Likewise, the redemptive story is grand and glorious because it reflects the greatness of its author. Who but God could be this good?

Amazingly, God has written the redemptive story in such a way that the characters in it can actually know the author himself, which makes him unlike any other author who has ever crafted a story. This seems true and well enough. But there is also something mildly unsettling about it. What if the story of our lives has not turned out very well? What does that say about the author? Can we still trust him? Why would we ever want to know him?

An Invitation to Theological Reflection

These are the kinds of important theological questions we must grapple with when we call God "the author." It is vitally important for us to explore them too. I fear, however, that the mere mention of *theology* might be intimidating. So before proceeding, I want to assure you that there is nothing to fear about theology as a discipline of study. The word itself comes from two Greek terms, *theos* and *logos*, which simply mean *God* and *word*. So theology involves words about God or thinking about God, which is something we all do.

For example, consider those occasions in your life when you slip into a deeply reflective mood, perhaps during a period of transition or crisis. You lie awake at night, restless and anxious, and suddenly find yourself thinking about God. You ponder the mystery, tragedy, and beauty of life. You wonder if God exists and, if so, what he is like and what he is up to in your life, considering the hardships you face. You think about the biblical story, too, and consider what it all means. You feel a strange mix of confusion, awe, perplexity, and joy. When pondering and questioning in this way, you are effectively "doing" theology.

It is profoundly human, normal, and healthy to think about such things. Theology is not just for the professionals; it is for all of us. Our responsibility is to strive to do it as faithfully and thoughtfully as we can. That is what I invite you to do with me in this chapter. With the Bible and two thousand years of church history to guide us, we will dive into deeper theological waters in search of the riches God promises for those who wholeheartedly seek him.

Revelation

The Christian faith teaches that we know about God because God has taken the initiative to reveal himself to us through his involvement in history. The technical term for this kind of knowledge of God is *revelation*. God is the author of the redemptive story (as we read it in the Bible), and he uses the story to let us in on who he is and what he has done. We learn that he creates, promises, judges, forgives, redeems, and loves. History — literally, *his*-story — serves as the arena of God's activity. We can thus learn a great deal about God by reading his story.

Authorship implies transcendence and control, of course. In that sense, God appears to be like any other author — Dante, for example, who wrote *The Divine Comedy*; or Shakespeare, who wrote *Hamlet*; or Jane Austen, who wrote *Pride and Prejudice*. The characters in these famous literary works (Beatrice, Hamlet, Mr. Darcy) take on life and the plots unfold (journey, tragedy, romance) because these authors shaped them according to their design. As sovereign

Lord, God does the same thing; he crafts the story according to his plan and providence.

The Author as Character

But God as author differs from Dante, Shakespeare, and Austen in one significant way—he wants the characters in the story to know him, which is why he has chosen to reveal who he is as the story unfolds. In fact, he wants the characters to know him so much that *he has actually chosen to enter the story.* Thus the author of the redemptive story, who stands outside the narrative, chooses to enter the story and play a role in it; outsider becomes insider, author becomes character. God saw where the story was headed, and it looked catastrophically bad to him. So he stepped out of transcendence and entered into time; he became a human being whom we know as God's Son, Jesus Christ. Moreover, God chose to write himself into the story in such a way that the character he became had no foreknowledge of his relationship with the author—Jesus had to discover and nurture his relationship with God as he grew up (Luke 2:52). His character in the story was that radically human. It is pure mystery how this could be.

You would think, of course, that God's presence in the story would have an immediate and overwhelming impact, washing over the story like a flood that consumes everything in its path. After all, we are talking about God here, whose presence is, by definition, obvious—or at least should be. The Old Testament provides substantial evidence that

God's presence was almost always noticeable. He created the world by his divine Word, wiped out Sodom and Gomorrah, divided the Red Sea, provided manna from Heaven, and sent a plague that killed thousands. God is power and holiness and light. How could God be anything other? How could God not be completely obvious?

But the Christian story does not follow that plot. God shows up, to be sure, but not as we would imagine. God came as Jesus Christ, the divine self-portrait in human flesh. He didn't make an impressive entrance. Instead, he became an embryo, wore diapers, and babbled unintelligibly. He had to learn how to walk and talk, work a trade, study the Torah, and pray. He grew up in relative obscurity, so much so, in fact, that the four Gospels say virtually nothing about the first thirty years of his life. After three short years of public ministry he died a brutal death on the cross. How God wrote himself into the redemptive story runs contrary to everything we normally believe about God. God as a human being? God born in a stable? God working as a common laborer? God suffering death on a cross?

The Irony

The apostle Paul grasped the brilliance and irony of it all. In his first letter to the church at Corinth, Paul explains how Jesus Christ could have used muscle to bully us into belief, power to intimidate us into submission, knowledge to make us look like fools. That way he could have demonstrated just how great he was, how divine he was. But Christ chose another way—humility, foolishness, and weakness. He served rather than conquered, loved rather than intimidated, forgave rather than judged, suffered and died rather than condemned.

Jesus did the opposite of what God is supposed to do. Paul writes, "For since in the wisdom of God the world through its wisdom did not know him, God was pleased through the foolishness of what was preached [the cross] to save those who believe" (1 Corinthians 1:21). We think God is simply one better than us, so we look for superior wisdom, superior strength, superior power. But in Christ, Paul points out, God reversed the natural order of things: "Jews demand signs and Greeks look for wisdom, but we preach Christ crucified: a stumbling block to Jews and foolishness to Gentiles, but to those whom God has called, both Jews and Greeks, Christ the power of God and the wisdom of God" (1 Corinthians 1:22–24). Paul's pen almost drips with irony: "For the foolishness of God is wiser than human wisdom, and the weakness of God is stronger than human strength" (1 Corinthians 1:25). God's foolishness exposes the folly of our wisdom; God's weakness exposes the fragility of our strength. We think we see God at his defeated worst, but that "worst" ends up being God at his saving best.

The Divine Dilemma

The incarnation—God in human form—dazzled the early church fathers, many of whom were converts from paganism.

Athanasius, bishop of Alexandria for forty-five years (328–373), viewed it as a kind of divine drama. God created humanity with the capacity to know, love, and trust him, and to share in the divine life as dry ground absorbs spring rain. But humans rebelled against God, which plunged all of creation—including every human being who has lived and will ever live—into ruin. "What then was God to do?" Athanasius asked, which he called the "divine dilemma." On the one hand, God could have condemned creation to destruction, but that would have undermined his original purpose, which was to share his life with the creatures he had made. On the other hand, he could have simply overlooked the problem, like an indulgent parent, but that would have violated his nature as a just and holy God.

Only one solution would work: the incarnation of the Son of God. God chose to solve the problem by coming as Jesus Christ. As Athanasius put it, "But now He entered the world in a new way, stooping to our level in His love and Self-revealing to us … He took to Himself a body, a human body even as our own."[7] Big became little; power became weakness; wealth became poverty; wisdom became foolishness. Likewise, providence chose personhood; power embraced pain; sovereignty gave way to suffering. It is as if all the light of the universe was reduced to the radiance of one candle without suffering any diminution, without becoming less than it was before. It is almost too much to take in.

On cold winter nights I think about the homeless in Spokane. I might consider leaving my warm home to work in a soup kitchen, but I would never seriously consider making myself homeless. After all, isn't the point to pull the homeless out of their misery rather than to join them in it? God chose to become homeless for our sake. Paul puts it so well, "For you know the grace of our Lord Jesus Christ, that though he was rich, yet for your sake he became poor, so that you through his poverty might become rich" (2 Corinthians 8:9).

Christ followed that downward trajectory all the way to the cross. Why such a death? In *The Confessions*, Augustine argues that Jesus Christ was the only person in all of human history who, as the Father's Son and equal, did not have to die for himself but chose to die for others. He made that decision out of pure love. Sacrificing everything, Christ experienced death to overcome death. Augustine puts it this way: "For our sake Jesus stood to God as both victor and victim, and victor because victim; for us he stood to God as priest and sacrifice, and priest because sacrifice."[8] The resurrection proved that what Jesus Christ set out to do he in fact accomplished. Christ's death defeated sin, death, and hell, the resurrection bearing witness to it. Christ now rules supreme over the universe. The main character in the story achieved total victory for all of us; then, stepping out of time, he entered once again into eternity.

Imagine …

I ask you to use your imagination at this point and to put yourself in the place of Jesus' followers. It is the only way to gain sympathy for the theological problems the first Christians faced. Imagine that you know nothing of the New Testament, nothing of the history of the church, nothing of creeds, confessions, and traditions, nothing of what is likely familiar to you now as basic Christian teaching. All you know is the man Jesus, a common laborer turned rabbi, and nothing more. You admire him and decide to follow him as a student would follow a teacher or apprentice would follow a master. Over time, you realize that the old titles simply don't work and won't apply to him. Jesus is different, though you don't know exactly how. He works miracles and teaches with authority, something the rabbis never did. You begin to think he might be the Messiah, sent by God to defeat your enemies and to usher in a Golden Age.

Then Jesus dies a brutal death, causing you to fall headlong into grief and disillusionment. You thought Jesus had been sent by God, that perhaps he was the Messiah. But like others before him, he failed. Perhaps he was an imposter after all, as his critics claimed. But three days later, everything changes. You hear rumors he is alive again, not as a resuscitated corpse but as a resurrected being who will never die again. You finally meet him yourself. You listen to Jesus as he asks Thomas to put his fingers into the nail holes in Jesus' hands and put his hand into Jesus' side, wounds that have already turned into glorious scars. You realize that Jesus has conquered sin and death. You fall on your knees, just as Thomas did, and call him "My Lord and my God," names you had used only of God.

But there's more to it than that. You have a religious background to deal with. You believe in one God who rules supreme, a God who has no rivals. But you just called Jesus by the same name. No Jew would utter such a thing lightly; in fact, no Jew would utter such a thing at all. You remember the thousands of times you have repeated the *Shema*, the Jewish confession of faith that declares God is one, holy, and transcendent. But here you are calling Jesus—a human being, someone you know as friend and teacher—Lord, a title reserved only for God! What are you going to do? You know it would be far more convenient at that moment to demote Jesus, calling him by a lesser name—martyr, rabbi, saint, healer, sage, even Messiah, anything but Lord. But by now that is impossible for you. Lord he is, Lord he must remain.

BIG QUESTIONS

The incarnation, death, and resurrection of Jesus created problems for the early church, largely theological in nature. These problems might seem insignificant to you, enjoying, as you do, a Bible to read and the cushion of two thousand years of history. But they were anything but insignificant to the first few generations of Christians. What were these questions? First, how could God function as God of the universe if he became a human being and suffered death on a cross? Did God cease to be God in the death of Christ? Second, how could God be one if Christ was God? Was God one or more than one? Surely he couldn't be both! Third, how could Christ be human if he really was God? As we will see, these questions are not purely abstract, nor are they irrelevant to daily life.

Question 1: How Could God Be God If He Also Became a Human Being and Suffered Death?

This question introduces us to the mystery of time. To answer it, we must recognize the difference between what it means for God as the author of the story to transcend time and what it means for God as a character in the story —Jesus Christ—to enter into time. Standing outside time as we experience it, God is present to all of human history as if it were a single reality; all times (in our world) are the present to him because he created time and transcends it. He experiences every event at the same moment, the entire redemptive story as one. God is at the beginning of the story and at the end of the story; he is the Alpha and the Omega. He stands outside the story, experiencing the whole of it as the author.

But as a character in the story, he lived one day at a time. God as Jesus Christ was born in Bethlehem, grew up in Nazareth, died on the cross, and rose from the dead, all events *in time.* Thus God's experience of time and Jesus Christ's experience of time are different, each meaningful in its own way. Somehow the two — God's transcendence over time and Christ's confinement within time, God's sovereign will as author and Christ's role as a character—fit together into a seamless whole, neither undermining the other. God envelops time, absorbing it into his very nature; he does not nullify it. God's redemptive plan envelops human freedom and action; it does not override it.

How human memory functions will help us, at least in part, to understand the relationship between transcendence and time. In recent years, memory has become increasingly important to me, largely because my kids have all left the home and moved on to other things. I see them and talk to them regularly, of course. Still, I miss them very much. In their absence memories have grown more vivid and significant, and the experiences we had as a family live on, if only in my head. I remember specific plays we attended during our visits to the Shakespeare Festival in Ashland, Oregon, meals we enjoyed, conversations we had. I remember John's many soccer tournaments, Catherine's performances as Maria in *The Sound of Music,* David's cross-country meets. I remember piano and violin recitals, family arguments, remodeling projects, games in the backyard, holiday celebrations.

Memory enables me to bring the past into the present, though not in the same way I experience the present itself. The one exists in reality, the other only in my head. Still, both are real, only real in different ways. But God actually *experiences* all times as the present, including the entire life of Jesus Christ. The experience of suffering and death is therefore not alien to God. God knows and feels pain, not as a single event in time but as an eternal reality. He grieves and weeps; but he also rejoices because he knows how it all turns out. Tragedy and triumph, sorrow and joy, are part of his very being. He is present to it all.

My son David is — and always has been — quiet and reflective. After the accident, he was the least likely to talk about it; but when he chose to, he usually had something significant to say or ask. I had to be ready to respond to him when he sent cues indicating he was ready to talk. Our best conversations happened in the car. One particular conversation has stayed fresh in my memory. David was eight at the time; we were driving to a soccer match some distance from our home. Typical for these occasions, David was quiet. The car was full of silence — not a heavy silence, but a liquid silence, as if some question was brewing inside him.

"Do you think Mom sees us right now?" he suddenly asked.

I paused to ponder. "I don't know, David. I think maybe she does see us. Why do you ask?"

"I don't see how she could, Dad. I thought Heaven was full of happiness. How could she bear to see us so sad?"

Could Lynda witness our pain in Heaven? How could that be possible? How could she bear it?

"I think she does see us," I finally said. "But she sees the whole story, including how it all turns out, which is beautiful to her. It's going to be a good story, David."

I would not hazard to estimate the number of times I have been asked, "How does Christianity address the problem of suffering?" People want some foolproof theological answer to explain and excuse God, and our answers usually come across as excessively abstract and cold, like a mathematical formula. The Christian answer to suffering, however, is suffering itself, Christ's suffering; it is also resurrection, Christ's resurrection—both of which are eternal realities to God. God knows pain within himself; God knows joy within himself. He knows the whole story as one, including how it all turns out, which is glorious indeed.

Question 2: How Could God Be One If Christ Was God?

The incarnation set off a debate within the church about the nature of God, and it lasted for over three hundred years. It is easy to understand why. Ever since the dawn of time, religious people have been inclined to view the divine in two diametrically opposite ways—as one God or as many gods. The former implies that God rules over all; he is one, transcendent, holy, powerful, and "other." The latter implies that multiple gods share power, each performing a unique function. It all comes down to one or many.

Then Christ appeared. Up to his death, people could fit him into a familiar category, as I have already noted: rabbi, miracle worker, prophet, Messiah. Then he died, which should have put an end to the story right then and there. But as you know, the story did not end. His followers claimed that Jesus had been resurrected, thus conquering death itself. They proclaimed him as Lord, which became the great confession of the early Christian movement.

They were right to call him by that title, of course.

But little did they grasp the theological problem it would cause. How could God be one God and Jesus of Nazareth (a human being) be *Lord*—the Divine Name in Greek—at the same time? As Jews, Jesus' followers believed God was one; as witnesses to the resurrection, they believed Jesus was Lord. Believing both, Christians faced the daunting task of trying to make sense out of the oneness of God and the Lordship of Christ. It was a new problem.

At first blush, it made no sense. If God is one, how can Jesus be God, too? Did God wear different masks, like an actor who plays the Father some of the time, Jesus some of the time, and the Holy Spirit some of the time? If so, why did Jesus pray to his Father in Heaven? Was he only pretending? Then again, perhaps Jesus was not really God but some special messenger instead—an angel or prophet. If so, why did they call him Lord and worship him as God?

Over time and through a great deal of biblical reflection, prayer, and debate, the church fathers came to believe a new idea about God—that God is not one or many but a tri-unity. Relationship is part of the very being of God. God not only *has* a relationship; he *is* a relationship. God the Father loves God the Son through all eternity; the Son likewise loves the Father. The love between them is so perfect, so powerful, so vital and intense and deep that it generates another person, God the Holy Spirit. This "generation" does not refer to a chronological sequence of creation, for the Holy Spirit is eternal, as Father and Son are. It does refer to relationship: the Holy Spirit is the living and eternal bond between Father and Son. God did not create us because he was lonely and wanted someone to love; he created us so that he could share with us the love that exists within himself. We don't make God loving; God loves within himself, Father to Son, Son to Father, the Holy Spirit being the perfect and eternal Love between the two.

God wants us to enjoy his divine love, to glory in it, to bathe in it. God invites us to fall "in love" with him, though not as we would normally understand that phrase. To be "in love" means we get *inside* love. It is less what a lover experiences with the beloved and more what children experience with their parents.

I discovered the significance of this truth soon after becoming a single parent. It was palpably obvious to me, of course, that my children no longer had a mother living in the home. Her absence made our home feel sad and empty. But there was more to it than that, though I could not quite put words to it. I sensed something was amiss, something other than the absence of a mother. It finally dawned on me that my children had not only lost their mother but had also lost the relationship between Lynda and me — our conversations, our conflicts, our affection, our humor, and everything else we shared together as husband and wife. That relationship had power to it; it functioned like a third presence in the home. There was Lynda; there was me; and there was the relationship between us.

That they missed our relationship became apparent to me many years later, and it came to me as a gift from a friend.

Perhaps ten months before the accident, a former neighbor of ours, Billie, visited us for a few days and, video camera in hand, captured scenes of the family engaged in the normal activities of home life. She decided to let time pass after the accident before sending the tape to me, which she made into a DVD. Watching it for the first time flooded me with memories, transporting me back some fifteen years to the domestic life of our home when we were still a family of six.

In my favorite scene, Catherine and David, then seven and five, are practicing a piano-violin duet, stumbling their way through it. Diana Jane, then only three, is sometimes pestering her older sister and brother, sometimes her mother, who finally picks her up and holds her. The entire scene shows an active and happy family doing ordinary life on a sunny fall afternoon. Then I appear in the video, holding John in my arms, and I greet the children. At that point, Lynda reenters the room and embraces me, with John squeezed between us. It is obvious that John enjoys it, for he puts his arms around the two of us, as if to keep us together and to keep his position secure. He likes the feeling of being engulfed. His primary desire is not only to be loved but also to be in love.

The beauty of trinitarian faith is that God invites us to share in the love he has within his own nature as Father, Son, and Holy Spirit, just as John shared in the marital love between Lynda and me. Theologians call it "participation"; it means that we can participate in the very being of God as a loving relationship. God loves us, of course, just as a parent loves a child; but God is love in his essential nature, and he invites us into that love relationship, which we experience as a reality quite apart from the love God extends to us. We get to be *in love*, not only as recipients but also as participants. We discover that we belong to a love that is bigger than us, bigger than any kind of love we give and receive; it is God's love, which we get to take in and experience. What John wanted and what my children lost was that kind of love, a dynamic love that existed apart from them, a love they could participate in and enjoy, like standing under a cool shower on a hot summer day.

Question 3: How Could Christ Be Human If He Really Was God?

If we assume that Jesus Christ really was — and is — God, then it seems a stretch to believe he could be truly human at the same time. How could Jesus be both? Surely humanity would have to give way to divinity as inferior gives way to superior. After all, God is God, before whom nothing can stand and with whom nothing can compare. Then again, how could God as a superior being become an embryo or have to learn how to walk and talk? It seems impossible. But is it? Is divinity superior, or is it simply different — different in such a way that Christ could be truly human, except without sinning?

Follow me to the garden of Gethsemane and watch Jesus in prayer. His friends are some distance away, and they have fallen asleep, weary and frightened and unaware of the chaos that is soon to sweep over them. Jesus is in obvious agony. His breathing is shallow; sweat forms as beads on his brow and drops to the ground; his face is contorted in pain, his eyes filled with terror. He wants to run away, but he remains rooted to the spot. He is there to wrestle. He falls on his knees and chokes out a prayer. "Father," he says, trembling, "let this cup pass from me."

He knows what the divine will is; he knows he must embrace the cross, suffer for the sins of the world, and experience separation from his Father. He knows all this, and he is repulsed by it. He wants to throw off the heavy burden and escape, perhaps slipping out of Jerusalem while it is still night. He can hardly bear the thought of the horror that lies ahead. But then, in an act of pure faith and courage, he says, "Nevertheless, not my will but yours be done." In that moment he chooses to surrender his will to the divine will, a profoundly human act. The internal struggle of human freedom and divine plan is resolved when human surrenders to divine, when self-will gives way to God's will, when freedom yields to obedience. Two wills thus become one — by human choice, not by divine domination.

The apostle Paul calls Christ the firstfruits of those who have died, awaiting resurrection (1 Corinthians 15:20); he says that the destiny of those who follow Christ is to be conformed to his image, the firstborn of many to come (Romans 8:29). As God's children, John adds, believers will become like him because they will see Christ as he is, which implies that seeing is not simply believing but becoming

(1 John 3:2). Thus God as relationship draws us into the love that exists within God, and God as Jesus Christ unites us with God and conforms us to his image as we see it in Jesus Christ. Further, God as relationship invites us to participate in his divine life, and God as Jesus Christ both invites and commands us to imitate his faithful obedience. Finally, what happens to us and in us results from God as Holy Spirit, who joins us with God, fills us with life, and empowers us to obey.

God is the author of the redemptive story. His intent is to reveal himself to us as characters in the story, which he accomplished by writing himself into the narrative. When we see Jesus, we see the author as a character; we see God as a human being. And we come to know and love and follow Jesus through the work of the Holy Spirit. God has done everything to make himself known, the perfect relationship of Father, Son, and Holy Spirit acting harmoniously to reveal himself to us and unite us to himself. There is nothing left to be done, nothing left that can be done.

Well, that is not entirely true. *We* have something to do, too. We must respond to God's initiative. I have already argued that though God is the author, we have a role to play. In this redemptive story we have real decisions to make in real freedom that have real consequences for how the story turns out. Thus, the one who wrote the whole story has created characters who have freedom and power to shape the plot.

One kind of freedom stands above all others. We can choose, if we wish, to know and surrender ourselves to the author, however good or bad the plot of our story happens to be. Though God transcends the story as sovereign Lord, he has also entered the story as Jesus Christ, author becoming character. We see, know, and experience God in the face of Jesus Christ and through the power of the Holy Spirit.

Freedom and Enslavement

We thus have the freedom to choose. But what kind of freedom is it? When I became a single father after the accident, it was clearly not a role I would have chosen for myself. Beyond the obvious truth that my children needed their mother, I was at best ill-suited for the role. Lynda was the real parent; I saw myself as her assistant. I smile often these days when I ponder the irony — no, the craziness — of the story. The parent least qualified was thrust into the dominant role.

There was no typecasting in this story. I had to grow into the role, fight my natural selfishness, and do the best I could, which often wasn't very good. I prayed a lot and kept at it. There was little "freedom" in such a life; if anything, I felt more like one of Michelangelo's prisoner sculptures. Over time, however, I discovered that it was within those very circumstances that I could find true freedom. My "sentence" as a prisoner turned out to be my liberation, my confinement set me free. I grew to relish the role because it helped me to grow up and forced me to turn from my circumstances to the one who rules over them.

Freedom has become a popular idea in our culture; it

functions like a doctrine that shapes our worldview and our decisions. We define freedom as both increasing number of options and exercising limitless choice. Freedom as ever-increasing options emerged with the market economy; freedom as limitless choices is rooted in popular notions of civil liberty. It is not quality of choice that matters, only quantity; not the right choice, only freedom of choice. Never mind the consequences! But it hasn't worked out very well, as we all know. If anything, these notions of freedom have often made us miserable.

The author of the redemptive story has given his characters freedom. But the freedom God gives is as peculiar as the story itself. It is not the number of options, not limitless choice. It is relationship with God and submission to God. True freedom consists, not in obsessing about circumstances but in trusting the God who transcends them, not in pursuing our own way but in surrendering to God's way. However bewildered we may be by the strange turns our stories have taken, we can come to know the author who stands behind the plot. We can thus plead our case, ask for help, and wait for redemption.

Such is the paradox of the redemptive story — we lose to gain, die to live, renounce to inherit, surrender ourselves to get ourselves back. We gain true freedom only when we surrender it and choose to know, trust, and obey God. The plot of the story unfolds in the strangest of ways: the characters in the story — lost, rebellious, and perverse — submit their will to the divine will, aligning their freedom with the loving intent of the author. In this story, the author releases characters to their freedom, and the characters in turn surrender their freedom to the author, making all things well and whole again.

CHAPTER 7

Time, Timing,
and Timelessness

It's your day off and you're sitting at a local coffee shop, sipping on your favorite blend while you try to read a book. For some reason you simply can't concentrate; perhaps it's the weather—it has been cold and gray for just too many days, which only reinforces your longing for spring. You stare outside for a while, then return to your book and read the same page three times in a row, failing each time to remember a thing you've read. You're almost hoping for a worthwhile distraction.

Looking up, you observe a middle-aged couple enter, buy lattes, and sit at the table next to yours. They appear to be waiting for someone. Soon another couple enters and, spotting the couple seated next to you, rushes over to embrace them. It is apparent they are old friends who have not seen or heard from each other in years. They all start talking at once, impatient to recount what has happened over the years. By now, of course, you have abandoned all efforts to read and have decided to listen in on their conversation as discreetly as you can.

They soon settle down and begin to reminisce, mostly about the experiences they shared as next-door neighbors —barbecues, vacations, school activities, soccer matches, holidays, even Christmas decoration competitions. You discover that their sons are the same age and were best friends through childhood and adolescence, the friendship ending only because one of the families moved across country just as the boys were about to start their junior year in high school. Before that painful separation the boys were allies in everything, including getting into trouble. "Do you remember when the police came after they set off firecrackers on the neighbor's front porch?" "Do you remember when they skipped school to canoe down the Little Spokane, using a canoe that they 'borrowed' and later abandoned?" They share memory after memory, laughing as they tell the stories of the crazy adventures of their two sons.

After a while, an awkward silence falls over the conversation. A shadow looms, as if the past was safe for conversation, the present not so much. "What good years those were," one finally says. "I am so glad Brad grew out of that phase. I can't believe he's married and in medical school. We wondered if he would ever become an adult. We are so proud of him now. Tell us about Skip. How is he doing? The last we heard he was working. Is he still at the same job?"

You notice tears welling up in the eyes of Skip's mother. She shakes her head, unable to answer the question. She finally turns to her husband and chokes out, "You'll need to do the talking."

"He's not doing very well. It's been very hard."

"What has happened?"

A hollow and painful silence follows.

"He's in prison," the father finally says. "Theft and destruction of property. He kept getting into trouble after Brad moved away. It was little things at first — shoplifting, for example. But it never stopped, in spite of our pleadings and warnings and threats. He fell into the wrong crowd and started to drink too much. He attended community college for a while but then dropped out, moving in with a group of friends we didn't know well or like much. He was arrested for a DUI. Then came the burglary and arson. He was caught and sentenced to three years. We're both heart-broken."

"We are so sorry. We had no idea. Your Christmas news-letters — well, I guess you wouldn't want to put that in a newsletter. I wish we'd kept in closer touch. Is there anything we can do?"

"Probably not. Well, maybe Brad could write to Skip. It might renew the friendship. Then again, it might make Skip feel even worse. We're desperate, out of ideas. We're open to almost anything at this point."

You notice that it is late. You gather your things and slip out of the coffee shop as quietly as you can. You feel guilty for eavesdropping on a conversation that began so happily and ended so sadly. You wonder what happened to turn these two sons in such different directions, considering that they grew up in the same neighborhood, shared the same child-hood experiences, and got into the same kind of trouble as kids. "Inseparable friends," you repeat to yourself. Now one is married and in medical school, the other in prison. How could this be?

Bound by Time

I am currently sitting in a local coffee shop called the Service Station, sipping on my favorite drink and typing these very words on my laptop. The sky is overcast; it is the coldest April in Spokane's recorded history. Conversations buzz around me. I am somewhat distracted from my writing by concerns about two telephone calls I have to make. This very moment in time is all I have. Yes, I am a product of the past; I carry with me the DNA of my ancestors as well as the consequences of all past choices. Everything that has occurred a thousand years ago and an hour ago now shapes who I am and what I am doing, at least in part. And yes, I also live in expectation of the future, which I am counting on and planning for. This is why I am working so hard to write this book instead of, say, waiting passively for a magical bolt of inspiration to strike. I know that all times are the present to God; but only this time is the present to me. It makes me wonder why I waste so much time *not* living in the present, why I pay so little attention to what is immediately at hand. Why am I so easily distracted by the past and future and so inattentive to the present?

Redemption is worked out within the framework of time, which is why it is important to examine how God functions both within and beyond it. The author of the redemptive story, who stands outside time as we experience it, entered it as Jesus Christ, his Son. He thus bridged transcendence and time by choosing to live in the same time-bound world we inhabit as characters. If we fully embrace a redemptive view of life, I believe it might affect our actual *experience* of time—how we use it, how aware we are of it, how present we can be to it. My hope is that a redemptive view of time will free us to be completely attentive to what God wants to do in our lives in the present moment, whether we are spending time with a friend, playing a sport, commuting to work, planning a lesson, driving a truck, sharing our faith, listening to music, or raising children. Since "here and now" is all we really have, I am curious to see if it is possible to be fully present to what is here and now, and thus not be distracted by what is "there and then," whether in the past or in the future.

THE IMPRINT OF THE PAST

I begin with the past. In my many years of teaching the history of Christianity, I have learned that history is a hard subject to sell to students because they seem to think it is about something dead and gone. Well, perhaps dead, I tell my students, but not gone, for the past exerts considerable influence on the present.

We bear the impact of the past in a myriad of ways. How different the story of history would have turned out, for example, if Constantine had chosen to convert to another religion besides Christianity or Japan had decided to bomb Russia rather than Pearl Harbor. I could provide a long list of similar examples. How the human story unfolds is far from inevitable. People make decisions that influence outcome, and future generations bear the mark of those decisions.

It astounds me to consider how different my own story could have turned out. What if my maternal ancestors had not emigrated from Holland or my mother had not married my father during her years of rebellion? I would not be here. What if I had not changed my circle of friends during my last two years at Hope College, a circle that included Lynda? Then I would not have married Lynda and my children would not be here. What if I had not visited First Presbyterian Church just once in the spring of 2008 and accidentally bumped into Patricia? Then Patricia and I would not have become reacquainted and married. Such what-if questions, speculative as they are, change nothing of the past, however intriguing they may be. We bear the imprint of the past as it is, not as it might have been. What actually happened is irreversible, and so are the consequences.

In that sense we are powerless. We can spend the rest of our days reviewing and wishing and imagining and scheming, but we will never be able to alter what has already happened. The past is simply there, influencing everything we do. The best we can do — in fact, the only thing we can do — is remember the past and respond to it.

Remembering the Past

That we remember the past reflects our capacity as human beings to learn, think, and plan. How we remember the past is something altogether different.

Take the two couples whose story I told at the beginning of this chapter. They lived next door to each other for many years and seemed to share much in common. Their two sons grew up as inseparable friends. Yet how they remember the past diverges dramatically. Brad's parents remember his antics in light of what happened to him in late adolescence and early adulthood; he finally grew up and made responsible decisions. Skip's parents remember his antics differently because he ended up in jail. It is the same past, but it led to two very different kinds of memories because of how things turned out. What to one couple was a symbol of innocent and silly fun ("boys will be boys") was to the other a harbinger of later trouble ("sow the wind, reap the whirlwind," "spare the rod, spoil the child").

There is no such thing as perfect memory, of course. We are bound to distort the past, however accurate our memory of the facts. We remember selectively and interpret what we remember to make sense of the past in light of the present. Thus Brad's parents think they did things just about right, tolerating his immaturity because he did in fact outgrow it. Skip's parents wring their hands with regret, wishing they had stepped in sooner, tolerated less, and disciplined more. We know, of course, that the world is not that simple. Brad's parents were far from perfect, Skip's far from inept. There is mystery here, for we can never explain why life turns out a certain way. Bad kids can come out of good homes, good kids out of bad homes.

Working Backward

How I remember my own past is a curiosity to me, especially the last twenty years. I remember that life was far from ideal. My kids didn't practice their musical instruments enough and complained when they did; they fought with each other, usually forming two-against-one alliances. Our vacations were often unpleasant; the kids whined a lot, and I was usually crabby at the beginning and exhausted by the end, questioning whether it was even worth it. There were tensions at home, struggles with friends, last-minute efforts to complete homework assignments. I worked too hard, they not hard enough in getting chores done. Even now, we sometimes fail to communicate well and thus misunderstand each other.

Yet, when we reminisce about our years together, we speak of them with gratitude and in good humor, often laughing ourselves sick. We knowingly embellish the stories too, because we want to cast the best possible light on the past and on each other. There is obvious delight in these memories. Why? Because our lives have turned out reasonably well, at least up to this point. Consequently, our memories are rich and meaningful, even when we reminisce about experiences that were unpleasant at the time.

Take my son John. He passed through a difficult period during his last two years of high school, which put strain on our relationship. I agonized over what to do and how to respond. He seemed unreachable to me, as cold as stone in winter, as impenetrable as a spring fog. At least that is how I remember it, though John tells me now that my perspective is inaccurate, far too dramatic, which again underscores the power of memory!

During his senior year, I got one of those dreaded middle-of-the-night calls from a police officer. "Mr. Sittser?" he said. "This is Officer Smith. I want to assure you that your son is just fine, and your car is too."

Who would want to hear such words at 2:00 a.m.—or at any time for that matter? He proceeded to tell me that eight police cars had just surrounded my son's car, and the fifteen officers inside those cars had emptied out and drawn their weapons. They ordered my son and three other boys out of the car and handcuffed them. An extensive interrogation revealed that the boys were in fact not gang members (what, my son a member of a gang?) and that the "weapon" concealed in the car was in fact not a real gun but only a new paint-ball gun one of my son's friends wanted to show off, inadvertently frightening someone who saw it when leaving a grocery store. Recent gang violence had put the officers on edge. In the end, it was all a big mistake. But it was no mistake to me. However innocent the experience, to me it symbolized my son's distance and rebellion. I spent night after night crying out to God.

Later that year, he left for college and began to change, ever so slowly (a process that continues, thank goodness!). Now a college graduate, John has become a solid and secure young man. He is studious and thoughtful, shows genuine interest in others, enjoys many good friendships, composes and plays music, works for a nonprofit, and loves Jesus. He is also engaged to Annalise, a wonderful Christian woman. His life as it is now informs how I remember his years in high school, which were, at times, miserable. The present actually shapes my memory of the past just as much as the past informs my memory.

Memory thus enables us to experience the past, however indirectly, as it unfolds over time. It can't change the past, of course; but it can keep it alive, if only in the head. In that sense it is a useful instrument. Without memory, we would become products of a past we can't recall and will never know, and thus strangers to ourselves.

Idealizing and Regretting

But memory does not always serve a useful purpose. At its worst, it can actually keep us from living in the present moment. That can happen in at least two ways. For one, our memory can idealize the past so much that we want nothing more than to return to it. We remember the ideal marriage we had until something happened that changed it all — say, marital infidelity or an untimely death. We remember the ideal family we had before one of our children became wayward or the kids left for college. We remember the ideal job we had until downsizing put us out of work. Those memories might be entirely accurate and reasonable. Still, what good is an ideal past if it immobilizes rather than inspires, awakens longing but never leads to fulfillment, makes us wish we could go backward rather than forward?

For another, memory can demonize the past so much that we wring our hands in regret and despair, wishing we could reverse it. We refuse to let go of an event, experience, or decision that had catastrophic consequences. It might be a child we wished we had disciplined, a foolish decision we made as a teen, a job we turned down, or a moral standard we failed to uphold, which had lifelong consequences. This list, of course, refers to wrongs done by us; it could just as easily include wrongs done to us. In either case, memory keeps replaying the tape, rehashing the decision, rehearsing the experience. We wish — oh, how we wish! — we had a chance to do it over again.

But the past is out of reach; we can neither return to it nor reverse it. It holds power over us because it is unchangeable, rolling over us like waves, one consequence following another. It creates the conditions of the present, whether we like it or not. Still, we have the power to choose how we remember and respond to the past, which enables us to engage the present moment in a redemptive way. How can we remember the past in a way that frees us to live — truly live — right now?

Redemptive Memory

It starts with redemptive memory, which enables us to remember the past differently — not as an ideal to which we would like to return or as a regret we would like to reverse, but as one chapter in a larger redemptive story we continue to live out in the present moment. God is in the past, however ideal or horrible; he rules over the past and promises to use the past, *as it is*, to work redemption. He makes all things serve his plan and fulfill his redemptive purpose. There is no Golden Age to which we must return, no hellish experience that consigns us to a lesser life. There is only God writing his story, a story of redemption.

The biblical story assures us that God does indeed use the past to advance his redemptive plan. The promise to Abraham and Sarah, which seemed — and, in fact, was — impossible to fulfill, was fulfilled against all odds; Joseph's years of suffering saved a nation from starvation and preserved his family; slavery in Egypt set the stage for deliverance from oppression and conquest of the Promised Land. Even the consequences of sin can be redeemed for God's good purposes. David committed adultery and murder, suffering a lifetime of consequences that cost him dearly. But the second child born out of that adulterous union, Solomon, became David's successor to the throne and a link in the lineage that produced the Messiah. Nothing is beyond the reach of God's grace and power. We can therefore trust that God will use the past to work redemption in our lives, which frees us to trust him and obey him in the current circumstances of our lives.

The experience of remarriage has allowed Patricia and me to ponder this peculiar relationship between past and present. Patricia married into a family rich in memory. My children and I speak fondly of Lynda and Diana Jane, and we also reminisce often about the adventures we had after becoming a family of four. These memories, as vivid and meaningful as they are, could have put Patricia at a significant disadvantage. If she had tried to compete with our past, she would have found remarriage intolerable, for she would have engaged in a battle that could not be won. As it turns out, she did the opposite.

Patricia and I hosted a backyard barbecue the night before our wedding for some sixty people. After enjoying a long evening of good food, conversation, and play, Patricia and I spent a few minutes honoring the important people in our lives — our children, my sister Diane and brother-in-law Jack, Patricia's mother, and our dearest friends. I then asked our guests to join me in prayer. But Patricia interrupted me to say that she wanted to pay tribute to one more person. I had no idea who that person could be. Much to everyone's surprise, it turned out to be Lynda.

Patricia shared her memories of Lynda — her work as the soprano soloist at the church and her role as the mother of four very young children, and she spoke of her with respect and fondness. She reminisced about the accident and the years that followed. She even mentioned one incident in particular: watching me go forward one Sunday to receive communion with my three children, all of us in tears, a broken family eating broken bread. She concluded by acknowledging her deep indebtedness to Lynda. "I am marrying a man and inheriting three stepchildren who have been profoundly shaped by this good and godly woman," she said.

In that moment, Patricia honored the sacredness of the past; but she also awakened us to the significance of the present. Lynda was a good and godly woman, to be sure; but she now lives only in our memory. Patricia is a good and godly woman, too; but she lives in the present as the person whom I chose to marry. She thus gave us two gifts that day — she honored a past we cherish, and she gave us reason to celebrate the present.

The Story's Outcome

Remarriage constitutes one chapter in the story of our family, and in Patricia's family story as well. Obviously, we are somewhere in the middle of the story, though we don't quite know where. Such is likewise the case with God's redemptive story. There could be many chapters left, or only a few. Whatever the case, we know what the final outcome of the story is going to be — the world's redemption, which assures us that God will use the entirety of the past to accomplish his good purpose. Such a belief will shape how we remember.

In *The Great Divorce*, C. S. Lewis tells the story of a busload of tourists from Hell who visit the outskirts of Heaven. Leaving behind the shadow, selfishness, and lonely isolation of Hell, they catch a glimpse of the light, goodness, and beauty of Heaven. While Hell shrouds everything in darkness, Heaven bathes everything in light, including the past. Thus, Hell turns what once seemed pleasant and happy into a horror, while Heaven turns what once seemed bitter and painful into a triumph. Lewis uses the story to point out how this process begins even during earthly life:

> The good man's past begins to change so that his forgiven sins and remembered sorrows take on the quality of Heaven: the bad man's past already conforms to his badness and is filled only with dreariness. And that is why, at the end of all things, when the sun rises [in Heaven] and the twilight turns to blackness down there [in Hell], the Blessed will say, "We have never lived anywhere except in Heaven," and the Lost, "We were always in Hell." And both will speak truly.[9]

The redeemed will see the whole of life in light of redemption. Misery will become blessing, confusion will become clear, desert will become living water, darkness the promise of a glorious dawn. All will be well and whole and wonderful, even what appeared at the time to be the opposite.

THE UNKNOWN FUTURE

So much for the past, which is always behind us. Now for the future, which is always ahead of us. As you well know, the future is as unknowable and uncontrollable as the past is unchangeable. In fact, the future does not exist at all except as a range of options and possibilities, none of which is sure to happen. There will be surprises along the way, no matter how prescient we are, how prepared we try to be. Looking back over almost forty years of adulthood, I could no more have predicted the outcome of my life as it is now than any of us could have predicted the fall of communism or the invention of the cell phone forty years before these events occurred. History takes strange turns, both globally and personally.

How can I make sense of my own story, considering how unpredictable it has been? At twenty, I never imagined going into formal ministry, though I became a minister five years later. At thirty I never imagined teaching or writing, though I eventually did both, and still do. At forty I never imagined widowhood, not even for a moment, though I became one a year later. At fifty I never imagined remarriage, yet here I am, a new husband with two lovely stepdaughters. At every stage along the way I thought I knew what the future held, and I was wrong every time. So much for control!

It makes me wonder why I — why any of us — try so hard to control a future that eludes control, to impose our will on something that doesn't even exist yet. How long before parents realize that, try as they might, they will never be able to dictate the destiny of their children? How long before entrepreneurs learn that they will never be able to predict and manipulate the market? How long before military commanders learn that they will never be able to plan the perfect war, knowing exactly what the outcome — victory, as they always assume — is going to be? We can prepare for the future, to be sure. Good leaders and parents and executives and commanders do that, and rightly so. But we cannot control it.

Most of us, of course, lack the power to impose our will on the future. We don't rule a big empire or run a big business or command a big army. Most of the time we just get by, doing little more than survive from day to day. How, then, do we try to control the future? By worrying about it, which reflects a kind of negative control, as if worrying that the worst will happen might somehow magically keep the worst from actually happening.

I tend to worry, which is probably a sign of my powerlessness. I worry about my kids—their travel adventures, their future employment, their relationships. I spent two years worrying while Catherine and Jacob lived in Bogota, Columbia, one of the most dangerous cities in the world. I figured that the effort I put into worrying would keep carjackers, thugs, drug dealers, and petty thieves at bay. Not surprisingly, I chafe under Paul's words, "Do not be anxious about anything, but in every situation, by prayer and petition, with thanksgiving, present your requests to God. And the peace of God, which transcends all understanding, will guard your hearts and your minds in Christ Jesus" (Philippians 4:6–7). I think to myself, *Paul didn't have any kids!* But then I remember that Paul had the church to worry about, which is even more burdensome.

What was Paul's secret? He had a redemptive view of the future, which put him at ease about what he couldn't control and made him boldly responsible for what he could.

Writing from prison, he spoke with confidence about the future: "For I know that through your prayers and God's provision of the Spirit of Jesus Christ what has happened to me will turn out for my deliverance" (Philippians 1:19). Did he mean deliverance *from prison*? It would seem so. But such is not the case, for Paul could not predict what would happen to him. He could only control his response to an uncertain future.

Paul continues, "I eagerly expect and hope that I will in no way be ashamed, but will have sufficient courage so that now as always Christ will be exalted in my body, whether by life or by death" (Philippians 1:20). His deepest desire was to live for Jesus Christ, whether as a servant of the church or as a martyr for Christ. "For to me, to live is Christ and to die is gain" (Philippians 1:21). Christ was the only certainty he had; Christ was the only certainty he needed.

Augustine had a particularly provocative and unusual view of the future, as he did of the past. He believed that past and future do not actually exist, except as forces that influence the present — the past as memory, the future as expectation: "There are three realities in the mind, but nowhere else as far as I can see, for the present of past things is memory, the present of present things is attention, and the present of future things is expectation."[10] This moment in time, therefore, is literally all we have, which means we must be supremely attentive to it. We have the freedom to be attentive as well because God promises to use past and future to work redemption, which makes regret and worry completely unnecessary.

Such attentiveness has to do with the little things — tasks, assignments, chores, relationships, responsibilities — that are most often and easily overlooked, largely because they seem so insignificant. If anything, the sheer number diminishes their importance. What are a few grains of sand, considering the astronomical number on the seashore? What are a few seconds of time, considering the expanse of time over the decades and centuries? Both my sons recently graduated, David from Duke Divinity School, John from Seattle Pacific University. I enjoyed attending the festivities that marked these rites of passage. The various events we attended struck a good balance between solemnity and playfulness. Typical of parents at such events, I took lots of photographs, kept the various programs, and engaged in many conversations with my sons' professors and friends. As I often do on such occasions, I felt sentimental. I cherish these times as glorious moments.

But really, they are no more glorious than all the small and ordinary moments leading up to them. The graduations were milestones. Weddings, recitals, championships, baptisms, funerals, birthdays, promotions, and anniversaries function similarly; they mark progress and change. But there would be no progress and change, no graduations and celebrations, no milestones and markers, unless we also valued and attended to all the little moments along the way. David and John read countless pages in countless books, wrote countless papers, and took countless exams, or so, I am sure, it seemed at the time. They "put in the time," as the popular expression goes, using library and laptop as sacred tools. The same could be said of musicians who practice scales every day to prepare for a recital; couples who do the daily work of marriage, remaining faithful and true, until they reach their golden anniversary and beyond; leaders who hone skills and develop competence until they rise to top management. It is not the peak moments that count so much as it is all the ordinary moments in between. And God cares about all those moments.

I am currently reading John Steinbeck's *East of Eden*, a novel I should have read years ago. My youngest, John, says it is his favorite, and he urged me to read it. It includes this curious paragraph about time:

> Time interval is a strange and contradictory matter in the mind. It would be reasonable to suppose that a routine time or an eventless time would seem interminable. It should be so, but it is not. It is the dull eventless times that have no duration whatever. A time splashed with interest, wounded by tragedy, crevassed with joy —that's the time that seems long in the memory. And this is right when you think about it. Eventlessness has no posts to drape duration on. From nothing to nothing is no time at all.[11]

The paragraph struck me as true when I first read it; but for some reason it also unsettled me. It occurred to me later on that Steinbeck left out a third alternative. Yes, there is "dull eventless" time, as he describes it; there is also time "splashed with interest." But there is also hour upon hour of ordinary time filled with meaning and purpose. It all depends on our willingness to be attentive to what God wants to do with it and in us — especially in all those dull and eventless moments.

I suppose we could say that the books David and John read, the lectures they attended, the conversations they had with friends, the hours they devoted to voluntary service while attending their respective schools were like that, dull and eventless. After all, not every book, lecture, conversation, and hour of service was scintillating. As it turns out, however, all those ordinary moments fit into a larger purpose. They had value, not only in themselves but also for something greater, which turned those ordinary moments into something extraordinary.

Throughout the centuries, many spiritual writers have addressed the power and significance of the present moment. One of my favorites is Jean-Pierre de Caussade, author of *The Sacrament of the Present Moment*. Writing in the eighteenth century, de Caussade encouraged cloistered monks and nuns to embrace every moment, however mundane, as a gift from God:

> To discover God in the smallest and most ordinary things, as well as in the greatest, is to possess a rare and sublime faith. To find contentment in the present

moment is to relish and adore the divine will in the succession of all the things to be done and suffered which makes up the duty to the present moment.[12]

We have no power to return to or reverse the past, no power to control or predict the future. We only have *now*. We can be confident that God is in this now, working his redemption. We are free, therefore, to concentrate our energies on what is immediately at hand. If uncertain about the future, we can pay attention to the little responsibilities that demand daily attention, like doing chores and homework, caring for family and friends, developing our skills and interests, and exploring the wonder of the world around us.

If married, we can devote ourselves to being the best husband or wife we can be; if a parent, we can give ourselves unconditionally and enthusiastically to our children; if employed, we can do the best work possible, even if our job is less than satisfying, the future far from secure. Whether sick or healthy, on top of the world or in the depths of pain, surrounded by friends or suffering from loneliness, we can be present and attentive to what God is trying to do in our lives, even when it is unclear or painful, or both.

What if there is not enough time? There will never be enough time if we think of it as a commodity to consume rather than as a gift to enjoy. The only time we have is now; the only task we have is the one set before us. Yes, past and future do matter, which is why we should never try to live only for the moment, as if we could escape the consequences of the past and ignore the significance of the future. We should not live *for* the moment recklessly, excusing irresponsibility and lack of discipline, but instead live *in* the moment redemptively, infusing time itself with timelessness and choosing to know, love, and obey God each moment of every day.

CHAPTER 8

Character
of the Characters

I like reading editorials. Over the years I have consistently turned to a few editorial writers who are my favorites, mostly because their perspective strikes me as fresh and insightful. One of those writers is Leonard Pitts Jr. In a recent editorial, he mentioned a conversation he had with his young son. Asking his son what he wanted to be when he grows up, Pitts was surprised by the answer. "Famous," his son shot back.

His son's answer reflects a major shift in cultural values in the last hundred years or so. Being known as a "personality" has begun to surpass "character" as an ideal worth pursuing. Historians say the shift occurred when public figures — artists, barons, athletes, writers, movie stars — gained notoriety for their genius and achievements. Many of their names are still familiar to us. They include wealthy entrepreneurs like the Vanderbilts and Hearsts, composers like Richard Wagner, athletes like Babe Ruth, activists like Margaret Sanger, movie stars like Ingrid Bergman and Rudolf Valentino, adventurers like Amelia Earhart, novelists like F. Scott Fitzgerald. In some cases, the public so admired their talent and accomplishments that who they were as people — their character, their moral behavior, their lifestyle choices

—became a secondary concern. Celebrity effectively freed them from the confines of social norms and conventional morality.

But Pitts's son was not actually referring to this cult of genius, which prevailed through much of the twentieth century. He did not say he wanted to become famous for some achievement; he wanted to be famous for its own sake, which we might describe as fame devoid of achievement. His comment illustrates a cultural trend to which we are exposed every day, so ubiquitous we hardly even notice it any more. At least Ruth and Bergman and Sanger accomplished something, and thus they earned admiration for legitimate reasons. No one would doubt the significance of those accomplishments. It is different today. People want to be famous for its own sake, which explains why athletes dope to win and entrepreneurs cheat to make money and people with no talent to speak of appear on reality shows and then hire agents to market their celebrity image. Fame has become an end in itself.

There is a reason for this little tirade, for which I only half-heartedly apologize. Considering this craving for notoriety, I feel compelled to ask two simple questions of myself, which I also ask of you: *What do you really want to be known for? What kind of person do you want to become?* The early Puritans urged believers to ponder their own death, which would presumably remind them of what matters most in life. It seems morbid, I know, but it cleared their heads of petty concerns and focused their thoughts on eternity. They did believe in eternity, too; they assumed that how one lives in time affects how one passes eternity. I'm not sure people appearing on reality shows think much about eternity, or even believe there is one. Perhaps for them notoriety is Heaven enough, which explains why they will go to such lengths to gain it.

It leaves me with an empty feeling. Would any of us really be satisfied if our faces appeared on the cover of some popular magazine, like *Time* or *People*, for no good reason at all? Perhaps a few would want that kind of fame; but most, I suspect, would not, at least not after a few moments of serious reflection. Notoriety for its own sake is simply not enough. We want something more.

That longing for more is intimately connected to the purpose of God's redemptive work. The story of redemption has a goal, both immediate and ultimate. The immediate goal has to do with two things: the kind of people we become in this life (the subject of this chapter), and the kind of influence we exercise in the world (the subject of the next). The ultimate goal concerns where the redemptive story ends — Heaven, which even now envelops earthly reality and promises one day to transform it.

The quest for celebrity, whether modest and local or grandiose and global, runs contrary to the good work God wants to do in our lives, which is to make us people of character and influence. We must therefore eschew the quest for celebrity and set our hearts instead on God's plan for human life. In short, that we are known for something is far less important than what we are known for. God wants us to be known as people who reflect the very character of Christ, which is achieved through union with Christ and obedience to Christ.

Choosing the Right Kind of Celebrity

Some twenty years ago I achieved the notoriety of becoming a victim of suffering. The story of the accident was plastered all over the local newspaper, and its severity (five people died) garnered some national attention. Our family became "the family who lost three generations of women" in one tragic moment. It only made matters worse when I wrote a book about it four years later. A few people even referred to me, somewhat sarcastically, as "Dr. Grief." It was not the kind of notoriety anyone would want, and I always felt uneasy about it. Two experiences especially forced me to ponder where my life was headed, or at least could have headed.

In the late 1990s, I was invited to speak at the national convention of an organization devoted to helping people deal with loss and grief. As a keynoter, I spoke to an audience of perhaps a thousand. I reflected on my experience of loss and explored the lessons I had learned from it, eventually drawing some theological conclusions. Afterward, dozens of people stood in line asking me to autograph my book and to answer their questions.

It was then that I started to feel uneasy, if not unholy.

Eyeing that long line of people wanting to talk with me, I sensed I was beginning to market my experience, to reduce it to a canned testimony, and to exploit it under the guise of "helping" other people. Not that speaking about one's suffering is wrong. Many do that very thing, and do it well. But there is risk in it all the same because it can diminish the sacredness of experience to the point that a quest for celebrity almost takes over. After all, no one stands above temptation; nothing is entirely safe from corruption. By the end of the day, I could not wait to return home; I had had enough and wanted no more. After that experience, I decided I would accept very few invitations to speak about the accident and its aftermath. Instead, I chose to invest my time and energy into two primary duties, both very local and very ordinary — being the best parent and the best professor I could be.

The second experience that caused me to question my life's direction occurred several years later when my kids and I spent a summer in Kenya. While I taught at a university, my kids served twice a week at an orphanage located in the middle of a Nairobi slum, an island of mercy in an ocean of misery. Most of the children living in the orphanage had either AIDS or a disability of some kind. My kids fed them, rocked them to sleep, and played with them. I visited the orphanage only once. During that visit I fell into a conversation with one of the African nuns who lived and worked there.

When I asked her to describe her life in the orphanage,

she detailed the rhythm of each day. "We rise very early and say our prayers together, after which we eat a small breakfast," she began. "Then we awaken the children, dress, and feed them. After our mid-morning prayers, we return to care for the children. We eat a very light lunch, say our prayers together, and take a short rest; then we return yet again to serve the children. In the late afternoon we gather for prayer, which is followed by supper. After feeding the children and putting them to bed, we pray one last time and then retire for the evening." She added that hot water and electricity are scarce, time off rare, supplies limited. Astonished by her description, which seemed incredibly boring to me, I wanted to comment about the difference between her world and mine, but before I could say a word she looked at me, smiled serenely, and said in a soft voice, "This is my life!" The tone of her words and the expression on her face said it all; she felt utterly peaceful and privileged to live such a lovely life.

When I lined up those two realities—the celebrity of my suffering and the hidden faithfulness of this woman's daily life—one looked cheap and tawdry, the other simple and good. My encounter with the African nun only reinforced the course of action I had already set for myself. Though I will never live as simply as that dear African nun, her example showed me the beauty and dignity of routine tasks and ordinary life—if lived for God. She achieved the kind of fame I want, which is no fame at all, at least not as it is popularly understood.

Seasoned Character

God's redemption, complete in Christ, is still being worked out through the stories of our lives. We are redeemed *from* something—lostness, brokenness, sin, and death; but we are also redeemed *for* something—intimacy with God, formation of character, and impact on the world. Do you remember the image of the weathered tree in the first chapter? It is a symbol of what God wants us to become—seasoned, beautiful, and strong—in short, people of character. It also provides a concrete way to think about the foundational question we are exploring: *What kind of person do you want to become?*

Defining Character

The best kind of person, I believe, is summed up in a word I have already mentioned several times—"character" or "virtue." These words are roughly synonymous, though virtue has fallen out of favor in recent years. Properly understood, character describes individuals who have influence because of who they are and how they live. They fill the room, not with a large ego but with intense goodness and quiet confidence. They typically demonstrate humility, good humor, interest in others, and generosity of spirit. You feel drawn to them and yet somewhat intimidated by them, and for the same reason. Their excellence awakens in you a longing to become like them, but it also reminds you of your shortcomings.

Virtue rather than character was the preferred word in the ancient world. It also appears in the New Testament (for example, 2 Peter 1:5); but character is used more often, most notably in Romans 5 and James 1. The Greek word for character (*dokimē*) and its various cognates describe it as something that is well proven, tested, and found true. It implies a refining process by which "thy dross is consumed and thy gold is refined," as the great hymn "How Firm a Foundation" puts it. Mature character reflects the character of Christ, who "for the joy set before him ... endured the cross, scorning its shame" (Hebrews 12:2) and thus "learned obedience from what he suffered" (5:8). To be a person of character, then, is to exhibit the qualities Jesus Christ manifested while he lived on earth, whose suffering seasoned him and whose steady obedience made him strong and true, like a weathered tree.

Character Transformation

Character transforms us, in at least two ways. First, it enlarges us as persons, making us bigger than our circumstances would naturally allow, for sooner or later all of us will encounter circumstances that threaten to diminish us, turning us into angry, selfish, slothful, or bitter people. God can use those very same circumstances to form Christ in us. I witnessed a beautiful example of this recently when I spent an afternoon with six couples who have been meeting together once a month for two years. They call themselves the "parents of prodigals" because every couple has at least one child who has traveled to a "far country" (Luke 15), forsaking the faith and values of their upbringing. The qualities I observed in those parents remind me that circumstances alone have no power to determine what a person becomes. Those parents could have become self-pitying, bitter, and punitive. But they weren't. Instead, they emitted grace and goodness and humility. Their suffering has enlarged and ennobled them.

Character also transforms us by purifying our personality. I define personality as who we are in our essence, through both nature and nurture. Some people are naturally funny, others naturally disciplined and organized, still others naturally adventurous. It is their nature to be that way, and there is nothing inherently good or bad about it. However, there is always a shadow side to personality. For example, funny people can dominate every conversation and treat life itself as if it were one big joke. Disciplined people can become insufferably serious and controlling, driven to impose order on the world, regardless of whether it is needed or wanted. Adventurous people can turn thrills into an addiction, taking unnecessary risks and neglecting relationships and other important matters.

Character refines personality — thus quite literally saving us from ourselves. It is like yeast that causes bread to rise, making it seem almost weightless; it is like salt that enriches the taste of food; it is like light that makes the world come alive with color. Character enables the funny person to use humor at just the right moment and in just the right way, the disciplined person to serve and organize without intruding and dominating, the adventurous person to inspire others to stretch themselves in healthy ways. Character infuses personality with the quality of divine beauty and transcendence. It is a concrete and visible manifestation of God's redemptive work in our lives, the "becoming" part of who we already are in Christ.

Acquiring Character

No one comes by character naturally. We aren't born virtuous; no one inherits character. It has to be cultivated, shaped through daily obedience to God as inspired and empowered by the Holy Spirit. We mature in character primarily through some combination of testing and training. Adversity tests us; hence the significance of the Greek word for character, *dokimē*, which means "tested" and "well proven." Adversity reminds us we are not in control; it exposes our smallness and forces us to reconsider the kind of person we want to be. The New Testament writers use one term in particular to describe the kind of circumstances that test and refine — *thlipsis*, which could be translated as "adversity," "affliction," "difficulty," "hard times," "suffering." No one would choose adversity, of course; no one would choose to lose a job they like or a child they love or a spouse they cherish or a business they own. But choice does not necessarily come into play when facing adversity. It simply happens, like it or not.

Still, adversity can serve a good purpose. Paul argues

that the "slight" momentary afflictions (*thlipsis*) to which we are exposed in this life are preparing us for "an eternal glory that far outweighs them all" (2 Corinthians 4:16–18), which engenders hope, for we know we will someday share the divine glory. But adversity also builds character, which is the result—or at least can be the result—of living for Christ in the world as it is. "Not only so," Paul continues, we can "glory in our sufferings [*thlipsis*], because we know that suffering produces perseverance; perseverance, character [*dokimē*]; and character, hope" (Romans 5:3–4). James argues similarly, using a word that shares the same root word with *dokimē*: "Consider it pure joy, my brothers and sisters, whenever you face trials of many kinds, because you know that the testing [*dokimion*] of your faith produces perseverance. Let perseverance finish its work so that you may be mature and complete, not lacking anything" (James 1:2–4).

Adversity does not have to be dramatic to have an effect. Strangely, I realize now that it has not been the grandiose events of suffering that have proven to be so difficult for me but the lesser disappointments along the way that have eroded my spirit, sapped my energy, and put me to the test. There were days my kids got sick all at the same time, or they started to fight on the way to church. There were the days my computer froze just before I was going to hit "Save," or it snowed a foot on a morning I had a 6:30 a.m. meeting. There were still other days I discovered just before breakfast that I had forgotten to buy milk the night before, which often inspired me to say a very bad word or two, usually under my breath, when driving to the grocery store in my sweats.

I recall another memory about the impact of mundane adversity, one I haven't thought of for many years. My son John broke his femur in the accident, which required him to be in traction for three weeks and in a full body cast for another ten. John was still in diapers at the time, which made it difficult, if not impossible, to keep the cast dry. It was certainly not the time to potty train him; as it was, he could neither sit nor stand. His cast had a small opening into which a diaper could be stuffed. Nights posed the biggest problem, of course. So every morning we set him, cast and all, on top of an air vent and cranked up the heat in order to dry out the cast. It was surprisingly effective, though it made the house smell like ammonia—a small price to pay.

I managed all this reasonably well until John caught a bad case of intestinal flu. He was a mess, and so was I. One morning I bumped into a good friend who was on a morning walk. When she asked me how I was doing, I immediately began to sob. Standing there, holding John in my arms, I was so distraught I could hardly speak. "The accident was bad enough," I blurted out. "But now this. How long will this go on? Will it ever stop? I just can't take any more."

Considering its relative insignificance, why did that one incident push me over the edge? The insignificance of it was in fact the problem. All of us face dozens of moments just like it every day; the impact is always cumulative, eventually wearing us down like dripping water erodes solid rock.

Mundane adversity, like any other kind, reminds us that we are not in control.

Not in control—that is really the point. Every experience of adversity forces us to make a decision: Will we stay on our own course and continue to be our old self, which adversity exposes as small and petty, impatient and angry, irritable and ungrateful? Or will we choose the course God sets and become a different kind of person, one characterized by love for God and neighbor, goodness of heart, and godliness of character? In either case, adversity will not allow us to remain the same. Either we will try to maintain control, growing increasingly angry or depressed in the wake of frustration and failure; or we will grow in character, becoming more like Christ. Every day we make little decisions that push us in one direction or the other, most often in response to adversity. It is these little decisions that matter most.

Fortunately, being tested by adversity isn't the only way to develop character. The second way is to submit to a regimen of training. The church fathers considered training preferable to testing, largely because it depends less on chance and more on choice. I've witnessed a living illustration of this truth recently as my sons have been preparing for a week-long bicycle trip. They'll soon pedal along part of the Columbia River and then down the Oregon coast. The trip they have planned is long and arduous. How they handle the intense physical demands of the journey will depend, at least in part, on how rigorously they have trained for it over the last few months. If they put in the training miles, they'll be prepared to enjoy the trip rather than simply survive it.

The great Ambrose, bishop of Milan in the late fourth century, used athletic training as a metaphor to describe how Christians grow in character:

> Can an athlete enjoy leisure once he has given in his name for an event? No, he trains and is anointed every day. He is given special food; discipline is imposed on him; he has to keep himself chaste. You too have given in your name for Christ's contest; you have entered for an event, and its prize is a crown. Practice, train, anoint yourself with the oil of gladness, an ointment that is never used up.[13]

How does such training actually work? We don't necessarily have to suffer the adversity of financial collapse before we acknowledge the bounty we enjoy every day, which is why John Calvin urged the faithful to practice gratitude and stewardship. Neither do we have to face tumult before we discover how desperately we need peace, which we can cultivate with a daily practice of silence and prayer. In short, we don't have to wait for adversity before we start to practice virtue. We can cultivate character in small ways—showing kindness to strangers, being generous in the use of our time and money, being faithful to commitments. This kind of training pushes us in the right direction long before we are put to the test.

CHRISTIAN AND CARDINAL VIRTUES

It is helpful to have a goal in mind. Character is a generic term, lacking clarity and specificity. The church fathers, however, made character far more concrete by outlining a list of seven character qualities, or what they called the "seven virtues." The "Christian" virtues (faith, hope, and love) address how we relate to God, the "cardinal" virtues (prudence, justice, temperance, and fortitude) how we live in the world. The Christian virtues establish the foundation for the cardinal virtues, which demonstrate how a vital relationship with God manifests itself in daily behavior. We might not always notice the foundation, but we can always see the building that sits atop it. Just so are the cardinal virtues grounded in the Christian virtues. In a sense, the "being" in Christ, reflected in faith, hope, and love, works itself out in our day-to-day "becoming" in Christ, embodied in prudence, justice, temperance, and fortitude. God forms us into people who look more and more like Jesus, who is both the means and the end of redemption.

Christian Virtues

The Christian virtues of faith, hope, and love are called *Christian* because they have to do with our relationship with God—who God is, how we know him, what we can expect from him, and what he expects from us.

Faith. Faith orients us toward God, enabling us to trust that God is true, good, and faithful, even when immediate experience—for example, suffering—raises questions about God's existence and goodness. Faith assures us that there is more going on than meets the eye, that God is true when falsehood seems to prevail, that God is powerful when we feel weak, that God is good when evil reigns. We know God is trustworthy because we see who he is in Jesus Christ, the divine self-portrait. As the writer of Hebrews puts it, "faith is confidence in what we hoped for and assurance about what we do not see" (Hebrews 11:1). By "do not see," the writer urges us to look beyond immediate circumstances to discover the God we know through salvation history and in the face of Christ. Abraham, Moses, Rahab, Esther, Ruth, and a host of others believed in God when it seemed absurd, and their faith was ultimately vindicated. Our faith will do the same. In the meantime, faith enables us to grow in character when everything in our circumstances tells us to doubt God's existence and to live only for ourselves.

Hope. Likewise, hope helps us to believe that God is in control of the future. Paul writes, "I consider that our present sufferings are not worth comparing with the glory that will be revealed in us" (Romans 8:18). As you know, suffering often seems to prevail in earthly life, threatening to drive us to despair. We are not alone in this, for Paul says that all of creation groans for redemption: "We know that the whole creation has been groaning as in the pains of childbirth right up to the present time. Not only so, but we ourselves, who have the firstfruits of the Spirit, groan inwardly as we wait eagerly for our adoption to sonship, the redemption of our bodies" (Romans 8:22–23).

Still, there is reason for hope; we hope because in Jesus Christ we see the destiny of the entire created order—his bodily resurrection from the dead, and through him the restoration and renewal of the universe, and thus the conquest of decay and death and a new heaven and a new earth. Jesus is the firstfruits of a great harvest yet to come: "For in this hope we were saved. But hope that is seen is no hope at all. Who hopes for what they already have? But if we hope for what we do not yet have, we wait for it patiently" (Romans 8:24–25).

Love. Love is the virtue that applies to how we live in the present moment. It grows out of the fertile soil of faith and hope, which free us to devote ourselves to loving God and loving others, being confident that God has acted in Christ to redeem us and will finish his work of redemption at the return of Christ. Love is not only the highest virtue but also the symbol and summary of all virtues. "Love does no harm to a neighbor. Therefore love is the fulfillment of the law" (Romans 13:10).

These three virtues orient us toward God and ground our lives in him. We have faith that God has been and will continue to be good; we have hope that God will make all things right, well, and whole; consequently, we have the security and confidence to choose the way of love. The Christian virtues affirm that we are new in Christ, thus freeing us to live as new people every day.

The Cardinal Virtues

Love expresses itself in the cardinal virtues of prudence, justice, temperance, and fortitude. The word "cardinal" comes from the Latin *cardo*, which means "hinge." The church fathers believed that these four provide the hinge on which redemptive life turns. They sum up what a redeemed life looks like, what God wants redeemed people to become.

Prudence. Prudence is an old-fashioned word that means discretion or good sense. Prudence should be considered the first of the cardinal virtues, for if we cannot distinguish right from wrong, we will never be able to become people of character, even if we try to act justly, temperately, and courageously. We must know what is right so that we can discern how to do the right in specific situations.

Prudence begins with the ability to exercise good moral judgment and follows through with a commitment to act accordingly. College students enjoy the heady challenge of debating abstract ideas, noting exceptions to the rule, and spelling out situations that elude easy answers, as if every moral problem is hopelessly complex. As they will learn, the moral issues that we face every day are more simple and ordinary. Prudence does not require genius, only practical wisdom.

Most of the important decisions I have made over the years demanded practical wisdom far more than formal education or technical knowledge. In most instances, I have known the right thing to do, even if I haven't always done it. As a parent, prudence asks me to put the needs of my children above my desire for happiness. As a professor, it asks me to strive for the success of my students. As a mentor, it requires me to ask good questions and to listen well. As a colleague, it demands I show respect, especially in dissent. As a husband, prudence expects me to love my wife as she needs to be loved rather than as I might want to treat her.

When I fail in any of these endeavors, it is not because of ignorance but because of selfishness and laziness. The ancient philosopher Plato famously asserted that to know the good is to do the good. But Plato was wrong—even when we know the good, we still don't always do the good. In fact, we rarely do the good. In most cases it is not information we need but transformation.

Justice. If prudence concerns the nature of right and wrong, then justice applies moral judgment to our conduct, especially to the ways we treat each other. Justice requires that we grant our neighbor his or her rightful due. What we mean by "neighbor," of course, can vary. The person living next door is our neighbor, but so is the person living halfway around the world, for both are affected, directly or indirectly, by our behavior.

In the case of personal relationships, justice demands that we show respect to every human being—strangers as well as friends—honoring them as creatures made in the image of God. I did not realize how poorly I treated strangers until I remarried last year. Patricia observed almost immediately that I tend to be impatient, abrupt, and even rude when shopping at a retail store or ordering food at a restaurant. She tells me I treat clerks and waiters as if they are mere conveniences, and she also tells me in no uncertain terms that it is simply wrong.

But justice must extend beyond the respect we show to our neighbor. We have a duty to establish a just social order too, which demands that we secure and protect certain human rights, as any civics textbook would tell us. Common sense alone informs us that we would prefer living in a world in which every human being has the right to life, the right to equal protection under the law, the right to education and opportunity, the right to live in an orderly society, the right to free speech and free association, and the right to purchase and own and enjoy material goods. We might disagree over what these basic rights should be as well as how they should be enforced, but not that such rights exist. As Paul states, "Give to everyone what you owe them: If you owe taxes, pay taxes; if revenue, then revenue; if respect, then respect; if honor, then honor" (Romans 13:7).

Justice also demands individual responsibility. In a healthy society, the process of teaching responsibility begins at home and continues in church, at school, on teams, and in any number of other venues so youth can experience the rewards of hard work and the consequences of poor performance. If we as parents, teachers, coaches, mentors, and leaders fail to teach responsibility, we only put off an inevitable—and likely tragic—outcome. The reproofs of life will surely visit our children or students anyway, and often in a harsh way.

Genuine love is not always indulgent, tolerant, and nice; it demands responsibility as well.

God wills to make us people of justice who strive in everything we do to uphold equality and fairness in the world. God made all people in his image, which is why we should show them respect; people also belong to and participate in the social order, which is why we should protect their rights; finally, people exist for a reason and purpose, which is why we should expect the best from them and hold them responsible for their actions. Justice, then, addresses how we function in the human community, how we treat others, how we seek their welfare, how we hold them accountable. Redeemed people labor to make the fallen world a little more like Heaven, which Jesus will establish in perfection when he returns.

Temperance. The third cardinal virtue, temperance, requires that we exercise restraint in how we use material goods and enjoy earthly pleasures. The Christian faith teaches that God created the world in all its infinite variety and glorious beauty. So delighted was he in his creation that he pronounced it "very good" (Genesis 1:31). Then God charged humanity, the crown of his creation, to subdue and care for the world he had made. Among other things, this means that our daily work — on a potter's wheel, in a bank, at a school, for a business, at home — has dignity and purpose. It actually pleases God, assuming we strive to honor and obey him as we work.

But recreational interests and hobbies can also honor

God. I have friends who are master gardeners, quilters, woodworkers, rock climbers, mechanics, musicians, and readers. My daughter Catherine and I kept bees for years, even operating a small honey business we called "C & J Honey." We enjoyed tending the hives together, harvesting the honey every fall, and selling it to our friends. I believe, truly, that this little hobby pleased God.

Temperance is primarily concerned with the problem of abuse and excess. It draws boundary lines that clarify when something goes too far, demands too much, or happens too soon. Temperance checks our natural inclination toward self-indulgence. We say people who drink too much, eat too much, buy too much, and play too much are intemperate, guilty of excess. But temperance addresses other forms of excess too, such as hoarding, wasting, exploiting, and abusing God's good gifts. People who build ridiculously large and expensive homes, who work excessively long hours, or who consume excessive amounts of energy are just as guilty of intemperance as people who eat or drink to excess. If anything, their excess might cause greater destruction because it is less obviously destructive and more socially acceptable.

In recent years, temperance has become the most difficult and elusive virtue for me to practice. Two decades ago, my experience of loss and pain awakened me to my need for God; but more than that, it reminded me of how many people around the world suffer. In my groaning, I joined a chorus of groaning that is billions strong. Over the years, however, the pain has diminished, the suffering abated, the groaning silenced, until it has become little more than a distant echo. Earthly happiness has given me a new song to sing. Not that happiness is inherently bad. Still, I face another temptation now, of assuming—perhaps even demanding—that life should always be just so, which turns indulgence and selfishness into a right. In this sense, my attachment to prosperity has quietly become a threat to my spiritual life.

The spiritual discipline of good stewardship is the practical expression of temperance. God is Creator, and the universe belongs to him. Though the world is his possession, it is our responsibility to care for it. God will judge us by how we steward his creation. We are good stewards when we manage and enjoy his creation, but not when we do so at the expense of creation itself. If we err here, as we often do, it is usually in the little things, which become habit-forming. We discard trash rather than recycle it, waste water or energy rather than conserve it, and accumulate things we rarely take care of. Or, in forgetting just how wealthy and prosperous we really are, we neglect the needs of the truly poor. All of these behaviors have a deleterious impact on the created order.

Temperance, then, calls us to live in the world as God intends, which in turn enables us to fulfill God's redemptive purpose. God created the world, and he placed us right in the middle of it as its primary caretakers and stewards. He invites us to enjoy but not exploit the world, exercising dominion as people who share a connection with the rest of creation but also share a relationship with the God who created it all.

Fortitude. The last of the cardinal virtues, fortitude, empowers us to face, endure, and overcome obstacles. Fortitude requires two qualities — perseverance and courage. We need perseverance to stay true to conviction, complete a task, and press on through adverse circumstances. And we need courage to face danger or opposition without flagging in zeal, wavering in commitment, or wandering off course. Both laziness and cowardice pose obvious threats to fortitude — laziness by tempting us to give up, cowardice by tempting us to give in.

Perseverance is essential for fortitude. But we need to exercise caution in how we choose to live it out. Ironically, it is possible to misuse this virtue by applying it in excess. It is common among many elites in our culture, for example, to pursue goals that require reckless fortitude — blind pursuits not informed by prudence, justice, and temperance. Such is the sin of many "high achievers," as we call them — students, athletes, executives, intellectuals, artists, and the like. They practice discipline and achieve success in some endeavor that, however worthy, compromises or neglects something more important. Simply stated, we must persevere in matters of true substance, in pursuits that reflect godly priorities. Nurturing a marriage takes priority over training for a race, investing in children over pursuing a hobby, serving the common good over achieving financial success. Perseverance for the sake of lesser things leads to idolatry. It must be subordinated to ends that honor God.

If perseverance keeps us going when we feel fatigue,

boredom, or frustration, courage enables us to carry on in the face of opposition or danger. We know it best as heroism —a bystander who jumps into a freezing river to save a drowning child, a soldier who takes a bullet for a comrade, or a leader who sacrifices his or her life for a noble cause.

When danger and opposition are severe, the need for courage is obvious. But courage is also required in circumstances that may not be so dramatic. One of my former students is spending the year teaching in a small high school in Africa. He jumped into his assignment with enthusiasm and worked hard to get to know the students and challenge them to do their best. However, he soon learned that his fellow teachers did not share his convictions. He started to feel their displeasure, which turned into meanness and criticism over time, perhaps because they felt convicted and exposed. Only courage will help him to stay the course rather than compromise his convictions.

Fortitude is like fuel that keeps the other virtues going; it provides the energy that drives us along the pathway of God's redemptive plan, sustains us when we face circumstances that tempt us to quit, and inspires us to heroic efforts and feats when we run headlong into obstacles and dangers that threaten to intimidate us. Fortitude keeps us moving forward as we strive to become who we already are in Christ.

The Architecture

Do you see the sturdy architecture of these virtues? Faith and hope lay the foundation; love supplies the motivation; prudence, justice, temperance, and fortitude provide the guidelines for daily living. Far from describing a "nice" person who breezes through life making everyone feel happy, these qualities describe a person of substance, integrity, and influence — a person who might make the rest of us feel just a little uneasy. The Bible tells story after story of people who exhibited these virtues. Prudence made Solomon a successful king, at least during his early years. Justice drove prophets like Isaiah, Hosea, and Amos to confront priests and kings for their abuse of power. Temperance enabled Daniel to resist the temptation of wealth and power during his years of foreign service. Fortitude empowered Esther to risk her own life on behalf of her people, the Jews. Jesus himself provides the quintessential portrait of true character. He is both means and end; he is the way and the truth and the life, which is why the New Testament says that the end of our redemption is to see him as he truly is and to be like him (1 John 3:2).

Once again I return to the question I asked at the beginning of this chapter. What kind of person do you want to become as you live out the story of redemption? I remember the temptation I faced many years ago to use my story of suffering as a means to celebrity. I am not sure I will ever overcome the temptation, at least not entirely. I wonder if any person can, for I have observed the same weakness in most people I know. We are plagued, all of us are, to feed the voracious appetite of our fragile egos, to angle for attention whenever the timing seems right, to acquire some form of celebrity even if there is no reason for it (which often seems to be the case these days). Is it really worth it?

There is another pathway to follow — the redemptive one. God uses the stuff of ordinary life to form our character. It might make for a less glamorous life, to be sure, but in the end a more fruitful and meaningful life, for such a life will reflect the character of Jesus Christ. God will use the many moments of dull routine and conflicted relationships and ordinary duties to grow us into creatures of extraordinary beauty, like weathered trees, each looking utterly, wonderfully like nothing else.

CHAPTER 9

The Spirit
of the Story

I want to take a moment to set the stage for the next two chapters. As you know by now, the redemptive story charges us to *become* new because we already *are* new. Redemption thus consists of becoming who we already are in Christ.

Both the "being" and the "becoming" part of redemption requires help from the outside, for as finite and fragile sinners we lack the necessary resources to become much of anything that is truly new, at least from a divine point of view. God promises to help us by sending the Holy Spirit, who unites us with Christ, empowers us to live for Christ, and transforms us into Christlike people. Through the work of the Holy Spirit our stories will begin to communicate a spirit that bears witness to *the* story. Who we become and how we influence others flows from what the Holy Spirit does in our lives.

But Jesus is more than the means of redemption; he is also the end. As I will show in the next chapter, our deepest longings point beyond this world as we know and experience it to something greater, to Heaven, where we will see Jesus and his kingdom in all its brilliance and perfection.

I turn now to the example of literature to explore how the Holy Spirit can engender a new kind of spirit in the story of our lives.

Good literature communicates a clear and distinct spirit, which is not the same thing as plot. In most cases plot is easy to identify and outline, spirit not so much. Yet we instinctively sense the spirit in a piece of literature, even if it eludes precise description. Spirit conveys a mood and transcendent quality that turns a piece of literature into something more than a story with plot and characters, emoting a power that affects readers at a visceral level, engendering laughter, tears, anger, or wonder. We find ourselves fumbling for words.

A friend says, "I saw you reading on the park bench yesterday. You looked completely engrossed in the story. What's the book about? What's it like?" The first question is easy to answer; you simply give a quick overview of the plot—mystery, tragedy, romance, thriller, comedy, and so forth. The second question is more difficult to answer. You might make a statement like one of these:

"I wanted to weep. The story made me feel so sad."

"It's the funniest novel I have ever read, though I can't even tell you why."

"It makes me want to fall in love again."

Good stories have that kind of power to move us, to tug at our emotions, to probe at the deepest places in our lives. They have a distinct kind of spirit to them.

Spirit over Plot

The spirit of a story has a dramatic impact on how we experience that story as well — perhaps even more impact than the plot itself. For example, we read some story with a plot we wish were our own — we wish we came from the same kind of family, experienced the same kind of romance, or enjoyed the same kind of privileges. Yet somehow the story leaves us flat and cold. We feel that something is amiss — it lacks the right spirit.

Then we read a story with a plot none of us would choose as our own. It is just too full of tragedy and betrayal and heartache. We would do almost anything to avoid having to live such a life. Yet somehow the story moves us, making us feel more hopeful about life. It has a different spirit to it. The plot of the story puts us off but the spirit of the story draws us in.

Isn't that why the musical *Les Misérables* has enjoyed such success? The plot is bleak — innocents die, injustice rules, heroes fall. Who would ever want to trade places with Jean Valjean? None of us, of course, considering the hardships he faces, the losses he suffers. Yet the spirit of the story continues to captivate and inspire millions of people around the world. Why is this so? Because Valjean's story conveys a *redemptive* spirit, which explains, at least in part, its brilliance and power. No wonder that the story became a model of inspiration for the kind of story our family wanted to live out. We long for redemption, and we can imagine how redemption works out, even under bleak conditions, when reflecting on great stories from the past, *Les Misérables* providing one great example.

It is vitally important to understand this distinction between plot and spirit in our own stories because each typically engenders contradictory desires. This is certainly true for me. I want "the good life," but I also want a meaningful life, which isn't the same thing. I want success, but I also want significance. I want my way, but I also want God's way. I want control, but I also want redemption. I fantasize a plot that makes me happy, yet I long for something more, too — something with beauty and hope and triumph running through it.

Sometimes in life we can have both the plot and the spirit we would like, but not always. Sooner or later the plot of our lives will take a turn we did not imagine and would not have chosen. Put simply, we will face surprises along the way — some delightful, others repugnant. What do we do then? It is this paradox that stirs up uneasiness in me. It makes me recoil from *Les Misérables* as the plot for my story and yet long for it as the spirit of my story. I don't want the disruption and drama of Jean Valjean's life, but I do want the beauty. The problem is, I'm not sure I can have one without the other.

It is the Holy Spirit who has the power to infuse plot with the spirit of redemption. He does this good work by uniting us with Christ and making us like Christ, which communicates a different kind of spirit — full of grace, beauty, and depth — in the world.

Aroma

In his second letter to the church at Corinth, the apostle Paul uses the word "aroma" to describe the kind of story that has a redemptive spirit to it, and he uses a Roman victory parade as his primary metaphor. In his day, Roman citizens scattered fragrant flowers on the road over which a victorious army marched when returning from a military campaign. The aroma of those flowers reminded citizens that their army had defeated the enemy, won the peace, and established security in the realm. Those same flowers reminded prisoners of war—marching in chains behind the victorious Roman army—that they had been defeated. Paul writes:

> But thanks be to God, who always leads us as captives in Christ's triumphal procession and uses us to spread the aroma of the knowledge of him everywhere. For we are to God the pleasing aroma of Christ among those who are being saved and those who are perishing. To the one we are an aroma that brings death; to the other, an aroma that brings life. (2 Corinthians 2:14–16)

Christians, Paul said, are like that aroma, whose spirit brings life to those who long for life and death to those who choose death.

Paul's own story illustrates the truth that no matter how tragic the plot, the spirit of a story has power to triumph over it with a life-giving, life-changing fragrance. Paul's plot could hardly be called happy or prosperous from a conventional point of view; there is no "guy meets girl" or "rags to riches" or "happily ever after" in it. Like Jean Valjean's, his story is steeped in suffering:

> Five times I received from the Jews the forty lashes minus one. Three times I was beaten with rods, once I was pelted with stones, three times I was shipwrecked, I spent a night and a day in the open sea, I have been constantly on the move. I have been in danger from rivers, in danger from bandits, in danger from my fellow Jews, in danger from Gentiles; in danger in the city, in danger in the country, in danger at sea; and in danger from false believers. I have labored and toiled and have often gone without sleep; I have known hunger and thirst and have often gone without food; I have been cold and naked.
> (2 Corinthians 11:24–27)

Who would ever want to live such a life? It is certainly not the life I envision for myself or for my children, nor is it the story I would want to tell in the family's Christmas newsletter. Yet there is a spirit to Paul's story that I find compelling and attractive. It emits the aroma of Christ; it conveys power and hope and beauty.

Spirit and Holy Spirit

I long for that kind of spirit to permeate my own story, and I feel reasonably certain you feel the same way. How can we get there? Does it depend entirely on our own efforts, our initiative and creativity and persistence, our faith and goodness? I don't think so. Paul reminds us that we are not sufficient unto ourselves for such things. In order for our lives to be characterized by such a spirit, the power of the Holy Spirit must be working in us. Paul links this work of the Spirit to the new covenant promise God spoke through the prophet Ezekiel:

> I will give you a new heart and put a new spirit in you; I will remove from you your heart of stone and give you a heart of flesh. And I will put my Spirit in you and move you to follow my decrees and be careful to keep my laws. Then you will live in the land I gave your ancestors; you will be my people, and I will be your God. (Ezekiel 36:26–28)

God's promise is that his Spirit will reside in us and transform us from the inside out. God acts through his Son, Jesus Christ, to forgive and redeem; he sends the Holy Spirit to apply these gifts to the believer's life. The result is glorious, endless transformation. This is how the apostle Paul describes it:

> Now the Lord is the Spirit, and where the Spirit of the Lord is, there is freedom. And we all, who with unveiled faces contemplate the Lord's glory, are being transformed into his image with ever-increasing glory, which comes from the Lord, who is the Spirit. (2 Corinthians 3:17–18)

This vision of transformation is no mere theological abstraction. We truly need the Holy Spirit, as much as we need food and oxygen and sleep, companionship and affection.

The reason is simple enough: we are not God, and we do not self-exist.

This truth became vividly apparent to me during a life-threatening experience many years ago. While backpacking in the Sierras, I came down with Rocky Mountain Spotted Fever. It is a rare disease, so rare, in fact, that physicians had no idea what was causing my symptoms. That I was sick, however, was obvious enough. My temperature spiked, my lungs filled with fluid, my heart raced as if I were running a marathon, and my kidneys and liver stopped functioning. The ICU medical team doubted I would survive. I was so delirious that the eight days I spent in intensive care remain a blur to me. One vivid memory, however, remains. I remember gasping for breath. No matter how hard I tried, I could not take in enough air, which made me feel profoundly desperate and fragile, as if I were one breath away from death. As it turns out, I was.

Of course, it is no different today. I am still one breath away from death. I just don't feel as vulnerable as I once did because I am healthy, which causes me to forget how helpless and fragile I really am. I need help from the outside; without it, I'm dead. I need air and food and sleep; I need encouragement, affection, and friendship; I need opportunities and mentors. I need God most of all—God as a real being, granting me grace and breathing his life into me, for God is the source of all good things.

It strikes me as strange that people who know they are utterly dependent on physical, emotional, and social resources outside themselves for their very survival still think they can manage on their own in the spiritual life. They embark on some quest to find the "god within," though they would never embark on a similar quest to find the "air within" or the "food within" or the "community within."

We are no more spiritually self-existent than we are physically self-existent. We need God. God knows that too, which is why he came as Jesus Christ to save us, and why he sends the Holy Spirit to unite us with Christ and nurture his life in us, making the spirit of our stories redemptive and triumphant. This is why the apostle Paul stresses the intimate connection we have — and need — with the Spirit:

> The Spirit you received brought about your adoption to sonship. And by him we cry, "*Abba,* Father." The Spirit himself testifies with our spirit that we are God's children. Now if we are children, then we are heirs — heirs of God and co-heirs with Christ, if indeed we share in his sufferings in order that we may also share in his glory. (Romans 8:15 – 17)

Who hasn't faced circumstances and responsibilities that force them to cry "Abba, Father" out of pure desperation? For some reason — actually, for a very obvious reason! — parents recognize this sense of dependence and need more than most people do, largely, I think, because they know easy success and smooth passage is simply beyond them. I would not dare even estimate the number of conversations I have had with parents who have faced such severe difficulties with their children that they have simply run out of ideas and options. They have nothing left to do but pray. As they often admit, too much has gone wrong in the past; too much could go wrong in the future; too much is wrong with them. And so they pray. They pray because they have to pray; it is pray or collapse, pray or die.

I remember with deep appreciation a discipline that Lynda practiced. She would slip quietly into the rooms of our children after they were asleep, kneel beside their beds, and, laying a hand on them, pray over them, asking God to protect, strengthen, and purify them, to make them his own. I continued that tradition after she died, and I urge the parents of young children to follow the same practice (and then to modify it when their children begin to stay up later than they do, which happens all too soon!). We need the Holy Spirit's intervention. Parenthood reminds us of that need every day.

THREE IMPORTANT QUESTIONS ABOUT THE HOLY SPIRIT

So far, so good. We know that we need the Holy Spirit. Still, what do we mean when we speak of the Holy Spirit? Confusion about the identity and work of the Holy Spirit is hardly new; the church has wrestled with it for centuries. Of the many questions surrounding the Holy Spirit, three are especially important. First, who is the Holy Spirit? Second, how does the Holy Spirit relate with our spirit? And third, what does the Holy Spirit promise to do in our lives?

Question 1: Who Is the Holy Spirit?

The first question concerns the Holy Spirit's identity. The Holy Spirit, as you already know, is one of the persons of the Trinity, joining the Father and the Son in an eternal and holy union of three-in-one. Still, Father and Son as distinct persons seem to have a clearer identity—more concrete and accessible—than the Holy Spirit, largely because the biblical narrative focuses on their roles and relationship. *Father*, for example, brings to mind an objective image. We know what a father is, and we know, at least in part, how a father should behave, even if we have not seen many good examples. Fathers have authority; they lead, provide, and protect. Rightly understood, at least according to the New Testament, they also serve, sacrifice, and suffer.

Likewise, *Son* brings to mind a concrete image, for we see who the Son is in the face of Jesus Christ, the "Word [who] became flesh" (John 1:14). Jesus naps in a boat, walks on dusty roads, teaches in parables, heals the sick, casts out demons, welcomes the outcast, and dies for the sins of the world. Then he goes on to defeat death itself in the resurrection.

The identity of the Holy Spirit is different. Nothing comes immediately to mind. Or, if something does, it is often misleading, inaccurate, even silly—a spirit that haunts people or a force that knocks people down and makes them tremble with fear. How do we make sense of the one person of the Trinity whose very nature eludes the same level of definition and description?

The Bible provides one prevailing image — wind. As wind, the Spirit broods over the waters in the creation story (Genesis 1), blows with enough force to divide the sea (Exodus 14:21), breathes down fire from Heaven (1 Kings 18), speaks in a whisper (19:9 – 18), gives life where death seems to reign (Ezekiel 37), and changes the human heart, turning it from something hard into something soft (Jeremiah 33:31). Jesus used this image to describe the Spirit to Nicodemus: "The wind blows wherever it pleases. You hear its sound, but you cannot tell where it comes from or where it is going. So it is with everyone born of the Spirit" (John 3:8). Luke writes that on the day of Pentecost, the Spirit came on the disciples with such force it felt like a mighty wind:

> Suddenly a sound like the blowing of a violent wind came from heaven and filled the whole house where they were sitting. They saw what seemed to be tongues of fire that separated and came to rest on each of them. All of them were filled with the Holy Spirit and began to speak in other tongues as the Spirit enabled them. (Acts 2:2 – 4)

As we observe in these and other passages, the Spirit functions like the wind, sometimes wreaking havoc, sometimes wafting gently, sometimes blowing with a steady breeze.

I spent six years in Iowa, serving as a college chaplain. Iowa is on the western edge of the great prairie, which stretches for hundreds of miles through the expansive Midwest. The wind blows there almost relentlessly. In the winter it can drive the cold into your bones; in the summer it can make the heat feel like a furnace; in the spring it can awaken the promise of budding leaves and blooming flowers, especially if it blows from the south. That Iowa wind was as unpredictable as a child, completely beyond human control. Such is the mystery of the Spirit of God. The Father speaks of gracious authority, the Son of human presence and sacrificial service, the Spirit of sweetness, disruption, and sudden change. As the "silent" person of the Trinity, the Spirit does not draw attention to himself but to Christ. Wind is the closest we can get to understanding his nature. The Spirit is power, mystery, and life. We know of his presence by the effect: union with Christ, transformation in Christ.

Question 2: How Does the Holy Spirit Relate to Our Spirit?

The second question concerns how the Holy Spirit relates to our spirit. The apostle Paul writes that the Holy Spirit bears witness with our spirits that we are children of God (Romans 8:15). Is there any way of making sense of this relationship? The most helpful analogy I've found has to do with how children acquire language.

My daughter Catherine spoke her first sentence when she was seventeen months old. I was carrying her from the car to the house, and it was late at night. Looking over my shoulder at a full moon, she pointed at it and said, "I see the moon!" That one sentence was as clear as the warm air that swirled around us on that memorable summer night. After putting her to bed, I thought about what had just occurred. It seemed almost a miracle to me.

How did she acquire the ability to put those four words into a sentence? Anthropologists argue that human beings are set apart from other creatures both by our enormous capacity to learn and by our helplessness at birth. The human brain is by far the biggest among all creatures in capacity, but it also requires the most time to mature, which is why babies demand constant attention and children need many years of development before they can live on their own as adults. In short, we have huge capacity but fewer instincts; we have a lot to learn, and we learn almost exclusively by interacting with the outside world. What becomes ours — knowledge and skills, for example — never starts out that way. It moves from outside to inside through a long period of development.

This is especially true of language acquisition. "I see the moon," Catherine exclaimed in wonder. That one sentence came after seventeen months of constant exposure to language. Catherine was born with capacity, but her brain needed stimulation to convert capacity to mastery. That stimulation came primarily from Lynda and me. We knew her and loved her long before she was born, and welcomed her into our relationship of love when she was born. We immediately began to communicate with her. Relationship thus preceded communication.

"Mommy loves you."

"What a big girl!"

"Are you hungry, sweetheart?"

"Why are you so sad?"

"Boat."

"Doll."

"Hot!"

"Dirt."

"Time for bed."

"Story?"

How many words and sentences did we say to her? A countless number. She responded to our communication, too, right from the beginning. At first she simply babbled, communicating to us in sounds that made no sense. Then she started to imitate sounds until she spoke her first words. These included words associated with relationships (Mommy); words associated with concrete objects (ball); words associated with sensations (hot); words associated with actions (see). She repeated those words day after day. At seventeen months she spoke her first sentence.

What astonished me most was the progression from external to internal, from outside to inside. Catherine would never have learned how to speak without us, for language did not originate with her. She did not invent it; she learned it. We communicated the sounds, used the words in proper context, expressed the right pitch and emotional tone, and repeated the same words thousands of times. Soon our words became her words, our language her language. Even so, language will never be entirely her possession. She will always be dependent on others to nurture her ability to communicate; left alone, her capacity for language will atrophy.

I believe the relationship between the Holy Spirit and our spirit works in a similar way. We have a capacity to know God, for God has created us in his image. Just as we long for communion with others — which is one reason we learn language in the first place — we also long for communion with God, even if we are not aware of it. As parents speak to their children, thus cultivating their capacity for language and relationship, so God speaks to us through the Holy Spirit. We receive this communion as a gift when the Holy Spirit unites us with Christ and nurtures our capacity to trust, know, and follow Christ.

Thus the Holy Spirit quickens our spirit to respond to God's initiative. I am sure you have had experiences of this kind, as I have — some pleasant, some unpleasant. A preacher is giving a message using a text from the gospel of Luke. She says something, and you feel your spirit quickened; the Holy Spirit turns the preacher's words into words *meant for you*. Or you are in the middle of a fight with your spouse. Suddenly you realize you are wrong. You try to brush off the conviction that presses down on you, reasoning that, though you might be wrong, your spouse is more wrong and thus needs to apologize first. But the conviction remains until you confess your fault. Or you spend two weeks one summer doing volunteer work at an orphanage in Uganda. While there, you sense deep in your spirit that you should start a nonprofit that supports similar ventures around the world. In each of these cases what is outside you works its way inside you, until the two become one. It is the quickening work of the Holy Spirit.

The Holy Spirit also fills us, as Paul describes in Ephesians 5:18. An inflexible object, such as a bucket, can take in only so much water until it is full and begins to overflow. But an elastic object, such as a balloon, can expand its capacity and take in more water because it stretches.

The human spirit is elastic—it can keep taking in more of the Holy Spirit and continue to grow. Thus our capacity for patience can increase, as can our capacity for wisdom, kindness, love, and all the other qualities of the Spirit's fruit. Our spiritual elasticity is why we can continue to mature into Christlikeness, "being transformed with ever-increasing glory" (2 Corinthians 3:18) and taking in more and more of God without ever possessing him, controlling him, or becoming his equal.

We are not—nor will we ever be—God. But we can come to know God better and become more like God if we keep being filled with the Holy Spirit. He is the source and gives; we are the receptacle and receive. God wants to keep giving; we must decide whether we want to keep receiving. This is why Jesus told his disciples to keep asking, seeking, and knocking, for his Father in Heaven, who is far more generous than any earthly father, would surely give the Holy Spirit as his most precious gift to those who ask (Luke 11:13). Thus the Holy Spirit relates to our spirit by taking what is outside us, namely, the divine life, and working it into us, as if working compost into the barren soil of our lives. The Holy Spirit quickens us and fills us, enabling us to know God through Christ and become more like God.

Question 3: What Does the Holy Spirit Promise to Do in Our Lives?

The Holy Spirit's primary responsibility is to drive us to God, where we find and experience true life. There is nothing like weakness to make us aware of our need for God, which is why the Holy Spirit exposes the foolishness and futility of living only for ourselves, an inclination that runs so deep in human nature. Paradoxically, we become most like God when we admit how unlike God we are—how weak, vulnerable, and dependent we are. In this sense, we are like the moon; we have no power whatsoever to produce light, but we do have extraordinary power to reflect light. We are —and will always be—utterly helpless.

Memories come back to me. I am sitting on the couch with my daughter, Catherine, then nine years old, reading her a story. Suddenly she looks up at me and says in tears, "I made mommy cry all the time. I was a terrible daughter." I realize that she is trying to establish order in a chaotic world, and she is doing so by taking responsibility for everything that has gone wrong. *Oh God, how do I respond to this? How can I relieve my daughter of this guilt and pain?*

Another memory comes to mind. Restless and distressed, eight-year-old John comes into my room in the middle of the night and crawls into my bed seeking comfort. This pattern continues several times a week for months. He is finally able to identify the problem. "I have no memory of Mommy," he says to me. "Catherine and David and you do. I feel all alone." Once again, I am sent into a tailspin of worry and bewilderment. *Lord, how can I help my son feel like he belongs?*

These were the kind of experiences that drove me to God every day in the months and years following the accident. But I wonder—was my life really that different before the accident, or did the accident only awaken me to a reality of which I was simply unaware? Was I more competent and capable then? Did I have more wisdom and power? Did I have the ability to control my circumstances, to make life turn out well?

We do have some power to do good things, of course. Surgeons deftly wield scalpels, scholars do research and write books, architects design buildings and contractors build them, mechanics repair engines, teachers impart knowledge. And they do all this whether or not there is a drop of religious blood in them—though, even then, they still depend, however unknowingly, on the Holy Spirit since it is he who gave them the talent and opportunity in the first place.

The fact is, we are completely helpless without the Holy Spirit, and we will have no eternal impact without the Spirit's help. Some things are simply beyond us, which is why we would be wise to pray with the psalmist: "May the favor of the Lord our God rest on us; establish the work of our hands for us—yes, establish the work of our hands" (Psalm 90:17). And to affirm this truth as our own:

> Unless the LORD builds the house,
>   the builders labor in vain.
> Unless the LORD watches over the city,
>   the guards stand watch in vain.
> In vain you rise early
>   and stay up late,
> toiling for food to eat—
>   for he grants sleep to those he loves.
>   (Psalm 127:1–2)

In work, as in everything we do, we need the Holy Spirit, who fills us with the life of God. It is the Holy Spirit who empowers us for service, convicts us of sin, leads us into truth, assures us of salvation, and reminds us that there is much more—so much more—to come in the future. We can receive these gifts, however, only if we acknowledge our weakness and turn to God for help.

The apostle Paul was no stranger to weakness. He writes:

We do not want you to be uninformed, brothers and sisters, about the troubles we experienced in the province of Asia. We were under great pressure, far beyond our ability to endure, so that we despaired of life itself. Indeed, we felt we had received the sentence of death. But this happened that we might not rely on ourselves but on God, who raises the dead. He has delivered us from such a deadly peril, and he will deliver us again.

On him we have set our hope that he will continue to deliver us. (2 Corinthians 1:8–10)

It is not Paul's admission of weakness that strikes me as unusual. Who hasn't felt such weakness at some point in life? It is his response to it that is so radical. Far from fighting or excusing it, he simply accepted it as normal and turned to God. "Therefore I will boast all the more gladly about my weaknesses," Paul writes later in the same letter, "so that Christ's power may rest on me. That is why, for Christ's sake, I delight in weaknesses, in insults, in hardships, in persecutions, in difficulties. For when I am weak, then I am strong" (2 Corinthians 12:9–10).

Paul's understanding of the work of the Spirit follows the same logic; he argues, just as his life experience illustrates, that God's strength is given when we admit our weakness. What the human will, weak as it is, cannot accomplish on its own—namely, obedience to the law—the Holy Spirit promises to accomplish for us in Christ:

For what the law was powerless to do because it was weakened by the flesh, God did by sending his own Son in the likeness of sinful flesh to be a sin offering. And so he condemned sin in the flesh, in order that the righteous requirement of the law might be fully met in us, who do not live according to the flesh but according to the Spirit. (Romans 8:3–4)

Paul reinforces this idea a few verses later. When facing circumstances that make us feel helpless and hopeless, the

Holy Spirit promises to intervene for us: "In the same way, the Spirit helps us in our weakness. We do not know what we ought to pray for, but the Spirit himself intercedes for us through wordless groans" (Romans 8:26).

The Holy Spirit also promises to make us strong. "When I am weak," Paul writes, "then I am strong." It is a paradox. When weak, we become strong; when emptied, we are filled; when powerless, we gain power. This is true because weakness, emptiness, and powerlessness force us to look for help outside ourselves—to look to God, the source of all power and goodness and love. And that is what the Holy Spirit promises to do in our lives—drive us to God. We will never outgrow our need for air, food, and sleep. We will never outgrow our need for God either. Never. We are and will remain as dependent on his Spirit to animate us spiritually as we are on food to animate us physically.

Prayers of the Saints

The prayers of saints provide ample evidence of strength being made perfect in weakness. Three such saints and their prayers come to mind: Aelred of Rievaulx (1109–1167), Martin Luther (1484–1546), and Teresa of Avila (1515–1582). All three accomplished great feats, mostly out of weakness.

The first prayer is from Aelred of Rievaulx, a British abbot living in the twelfth century who wrote an influential book called *On Spiritual Friendship*:

Lord, I sometimes wander away from you. But this is not because I am deliberately turning my back on you. It is because of the inconstancy of my mind. I weaken in my intention to give my whole soul to you. I fall back into thinking of myself as my own master. But when I wander from you, my life becomes a burden, and within me I find nothing but darkness and wretchedness, fear and anxiety. So I come back to you, and confess that I have sinned against you. And I know you will forgive me.[14]

The second comes from Martin Luther, the great German reformer who spent the better part of his adult life in constant conflict with ecclesiastical and political authorities.

Behold, Lord, an empty vessel that needs to be filled. My Lord, fill it. I am weak in the faith; strengthen me. I am cold in love; warm me and make me fervent that my love may go out to my neighbor. I do not have a strong and firm faith; at times I doubt and am unable to trust you altogether. O Lord, help me. Strengthen my faith and trust in you. In you I have sealed the treasures of all I have. I am poor; you are rich and came to be merciful to the poor. I am a sinner; you are upright. With me there is an abundance of sin; in you is the fullness of righteousness. Therefore, I will remain with you, of whom I can receive, but to whom I may not give. Amen.[15]

The third example comes from the pen of Teresa of Avila, a sixteenth-century reformer of Spanish Catholicism.

How is it, my God, that you have given me this hectic busy life when I have so little time to enjoy your presence? Throughout the day people are waiting to speak with me, and even at meals I have to continue talking to people about their needs and problems. During sleep itself I am still thinking and dreaming about the multitude of concerns that surround me. I do all this not for my own sake, but for yours. To me my present pattern of life is a torment; I only hope that for you it is truly a sacrifice of love. I know that you are constantly beside me, yet I am usually so busy that I ignore you. If you want me to remain so busy, please force me to think about and love you even in the midst of such hectic activity. If you do not want me so busy, please release me from it, showing how others can take over my responsibilities.[16]

In each case weakness, so obviously exposed through conflict and suffering, so freely confessed in prayer, made these people open and eager to receive God's good gifts. Empty, they asked to be filled; desperate, they sought God's assistance; broken, they pleaded for wholeness. The Holy Spirit quickened and filled them. We are the heirs and beneficiaries of their good work.

The Blessing

A recent experience I had provides still another example of how the Holy Spirit bestows strength in moments of human weakness. I have already mentioned my son David's graduation from Duke Divinity School. The experience of that day was everything that I had expected, and then some. What occurred the next day, however, was something I did not at all expect. One of David's good friends was to be ordained at a rural Baptist church. It was an event David did not want to miss. So David, his girlfriend (now wife) Kelli, Patricia, and I drove an hour through North Carolina until we reached a small church situated in the middle of farm country.

On our arrival, the usher asked us to sit in the pews to the left, where Tyler's family and friends were already seated. The sanctuary was simple and homey, a perfect match for its rural setting. Laypeople presided over most of the service. Some prayed; others delivered a charge; still others reflected on Tyler's work there, demonstrating how beloved he was. One woman presented Tyler with a Bible to remind him of his duty to proclaim the Word "in season and out of season," a framed copy of his ordination certificate to mark the special day, and a basin and towel to encourage him to serve as Christ did. The pastor's message was worthy of any pulpit in America, and the twelve-member choir sang with so much heart it could easily have passed for a choir of fifty.

Up to that point, the ordination service was meaningful but not unusual. All that changed when the pastor asked Tyler to stand up and, handing him a pillow, to kneel before the congregation. I assumed at this point that the pastor and possibly the elders would pray for him. I could not have been more wrong. The pastor invited every person present

—young and old, member and visitor—to file by Tyler, lay hands on him, say a private word to him or pray over him. Kneeling in submission and weakness, head bowed and eyes closed, Tyler received the congregation's blessing—word after word, prayer upon prayer, tears and smiles and hugs, cascading down upon him in a torrent of love. Tyler did not stop weeping for half an hour or more, so overwhelmed was he by this expression of love. God was clearly present in that sanctuary, blowing the wind of the Holy Spirit's life and power into Tyler through the people who cared for him so deeply.

I don't know what will become of Tyler, or what he will do with the blessing he received through that ordination service. That he did receive blessing from God was evident to all, including Tyler, whose sense of unworthiness and weakness was swallowed up by the dignity of his calling, the congregation's love for him, and the anointing of God. On that day, at least, his spirit and the Holy Spirit were joined. In future years he could choose to neglect the experience, thinking himself sufficient to do God's work without God's help; or he could also cherish it, knowing he will never be able to bear fruit of any kind apart from the power of God. Either way, he will not forget it, and neither will those of us who were there.

My children are now grown and gone, and I am remarried. If the story were to end today, we would be able to say that it had a happy ending. Still, a "happy ending" refers mostly to plot. I am more interested in the spirit of the story.

What kind of fragrance does my story emit? What kind of impression will it leave? What kind of impact will it have on others? Will it bring to mind God's goodness? Will it build faith, stir up hope, and inspire obedience to God? Will it call people to renew their commitment to God? Will it have a redemptive impact on others?

My natural inclination is to assert control as best I can. However, as my story so graphically illustrates, I have had scant success in such endeavors. My powers are severely limited, and I suspect that is true for you as well, not only in shaping the plot as we would like but also in engendering the right kind of spirit. The best you and I can do — the only thing we can do, really — is to invite the Holy Spirit to unite us with Christ, to make us like Christ, and to impart divine life in us, producing a beautiful aroma that will awaken people to the reality of God, to the power of the kingdom, and to the promise of an eternal spring.

CHAPTER 10

The End
and the Beginning

Every year I buy myself a Christmas present—a calendar I hang on the pantry door so I can keep track of important events, such as midweek appointments and meetings, weekend visits, and weekends away. Its central location is important because it keeps the family schedule right before my eyes, sparing me from double-booking myself, an error I have committed on too many occasions. But it also provides an excuse to display a monthly photo of some beautiful scene from nature. I prefer calendars printed by National Geographic or the Sierra Club for that very reason. I tried Castles of Europe one year, Pubs of Ireland, and Famous Lighthouses. But I grew tired of the photos by the second week. There's nothing quite like a desert or waterfall or mountain range to hold interest to the last day of the month.

Over the years, a number of stunningly beautiful photos have appeared on that pantry door. One photo in particular, however, lingers in my memory, a photo of the California coast. A rocky cliff, shaped like a half moon and teeming with vegetation, surrounds a little cove and then juts out into the ocean, making the scene feel private and pristine, like an undiscovered hideaway. A ribbon of a waterfall tumbles gently over the cliff and onto a sandy beach, where it meanders its way to the ocean. It seems the perfect place for lovers to enjoy a summer picnic.

For the entire month, my kids and I could not stop staring at that photo. It had a mystical quality to it—lovely, mysterious, and enchanting. It awakened in all of us a deep, almost holy desire to see and experience the place for ourselves—which we did, quite by accident, two years later.

Driving down the California coast along the Pacific Coast Highway on one of our yearly summer vacations, we decided to enjoy a leisurely picnic at a spot that, rising a few hundred feet above the beach, provided a glorious view of the coast and ocean. We took some time to explore the area after lunch, wandering down a trail that beckoned us to follow. I think it was David who came upon the place first, and he called frantically for us to catch up with him. "I found it! I found it!"

As you can guess by now, it was the very cove, cliff, beach, and waterfall we had gazed upon so longingly in the calendar photograph. But our experience of the scene was very different from the photo, as different as three dimensions are from two. In addition to seeing it, now we could smell it, hear it, feel it, and explore it. The photo depicted something real, though it was not the thing itself. The actual experience was so much better.

I will never forget the pure delight of hearing David's cry of discovery and seeing the place for myself. It seemed almost supernatural, for a longing was finally fulfilled, a picture of something we loved became the thing itself. I have often thought about that experience in the years since. What if our experience of life in the world is something like viewing a two-dimensional photo, but moving closer every day to a three-dimensional transformation? I suppose we could assume that the photo of life as we see it is all there is. But there is enough evidence in this world to make us reconsider —hints of something more, something bigger and better and grander, a reality that does not nullify this world but instead envelopes it, as three dimensions envelop two.

LONGING FOR MORE

I am curious about this human longing for something more. We long for so many things—beauty, joy, and love; good health and harmonious relationships; meaningful work; peace and plenty in the world; life after death. *Where do these longings come from?* It is a compelling question. You would think by now that the misery of human existence would have long ago led us to dismiss such longings and accept the inevitable suffering and death that awaits us all. "Vanity of vanities, all is vanity," writes the author of Ecclesiastes.

So what is it that keeps these longings alive? Why do we resist the notion that life in this world is all there is? The apostle Paul suggests that all of creation is groaning for this "something more," as if this longing were implanted in the very soul of the entire created order (Romans 8:22). We see and experience the fallenness of the world, but we refuse to believe it is ultimate and final. We know it can and should be different. How strange this longing is.

Tomorrow is Diana Jane's birthday. She would be twenty-four years old. I think about her every day, and I am especially mindful of her on occasions like Christmas, the anniversary of the accident, and her birthday. That she died prematurely is not especially unusual. Many people die before they reach old age, and those who do reach old age usually suffer many losses along the way. Why do I still mourn her absence and think about her so often? Why do I miss her and yearn for her? Why do I sense that our relationship has not ended, though she is no longer here? It could be just so much wishful thinking, a matter of pure sentimentality and fatherly emotion, a vain attempt to keep her with me, though she is forever gone. But it could be something else, too.

Tomorrow I will write my children an email, which I do on every important anniversary, and celebrate the gift that Diana Jane was and still is to us. I will remind them that the few short years we had with her were pure gift, and I will tell them that the story is not over yet—hers as well as ours. There is more going on than meets the eye, a larger reality that envelops the reality of our immediate experience.

Longing for Heaven

We are right to think this way, too. I believe that all of our longings point to an ultimate longing, which is the longing for Heaven. We long for Heaven because it is real, as real as the scene captured in the photo hanging on our pantry door. We live in two dimensions but know there are three; we see in black and white but know there is color; we live in shadow but know there is substance and light. Heaven is the ultimate destination toward which every one of our redemptive stories is moving. The little "heavens" we might experience along the way are mere glimpses of the true Heaven, tastes of the final banquet, signs that point to something real and eternal.

I should probably explain what I mean by Heaven. Heaven is the rule of God over all of life in and through Jesus Christ. God is supreme, sovereign over the universe. He has created the universe, and he has acted to redeem the universe, making it whole and harmonious. We know that God has acted because his Son Jesus Christ invaded this world and secured through his death and resurrection a beachhead for God's kingdom. God continues to expand that beachhead through the power of the Holy Spirit and through the ministry of his people, the church. He won't quit reclaiming territory until all of creation is restored and renewed. The decisive battle has been won, though the war continues (coming to an end only when Jesus himself returns). Eventually, God will establish his rule over all of life, and his reign and realm will become one. Just so will Heaven come to earth, making all things well and whole. Heaven is thus the realization and fulfillment of our relationship with Christ. He who is means becomes end; he who is source of life becomes life itself, finally and completely.

Heaven is thus not some "place" out there, as if it were in another solar system or galaxy. It envelops earth as three dimensions envelop two. When we see and experience it for ourselves, we will become aware of how big, grand, and glorious it is in comparison to our life in this world. Whatever good there is in the old life will be swallowed up, completed and perfected in the next, just as the calendar photo hanging on the pantry door was swallowed up by the beauty and grandeur of the real thing. All this will happen because of who is there; we will see God in the face of Jesus Christ.

Glimpses

We can see glimpses of Heaven now, as if looking through a portal; but they are only that — glimpses. The miracles of Jesus provide such a glimpse. Take the story of Lazarus (John 11). For a long time I assumed that the real point of the story was the raising of Lazarus. He had died, and Jesus raised him from the dead. Simple enough. Who wouldn't want to experience such a miracle?

But then it occurred to me that a miracle, however impressive, didn't solve the real problem for Lazarus and his family. Lazarus was resuscitated, to be sure, a glorious miracle; but Lazarus eventually died again. The story does not tell us when or how. Perhaps he died two years later of a heart attack or ten years later of cancer; perhaps he suffered horribly before that second death, putting incredible stress on his family. Is this the best Jesus can do? Is his power limited to postponing the inevitable?

Mary and Martha knew Jesus well. When Lazarus fell ill, they naturally summoned their friend Jesus to heal Lazarus, and they had good reason to believe Jesus could—and would—perform a miracle. Strangely, Jesus waited two days before traveling to Bethany, the small town in which they lived. By the time he arrived, Lazarus had been dead four days, a phrase repeated twice in the story to show Lazarus was dead beyond any hope of a miracle.

When Martha heard Jesus was near, she left grieving family and friends to meet him. Far from greeting him warmly, she said, both accusingly and pleadingly, "Lord ... if you had been here, my brother would not have died" (John 11:21). Which was true enough. Lazarus would probably not have died if Jesus had arrived on time, for Jesus had the power to heal sick people, as he demonstrated so many times. Jesus assured Martha that her brother would rise again, which Martha interpreted as an event that would happen "at the last day." Only then did Jesus tell Martha of the real miracle toward which all miracles point. It was not the resuscitation of Lazarus but something far better. "I am the resurrection and the life," he said to her. "The one who believes in me will live, even though they die; and whoever lives by believing in me will never die" (John 11:25–26).

Martha returned to her home and told Mary that Jesus had arrived. Mary also rushed to see him, as her sister Martha had, and repeated Martha's words, "Lord, if you had been here, my brother would not have died" (John 11:32), which indicates that the two sisters had shared their grievances with each other. After weeping for a while with Mary, Jesus proceeded to the tomb and asked bystanders to roll the stone away from the cave's opening. Jesus prayed and then commanded Lazarus to come forth from the grave. Lazarus obeyed the command, though he was dead when Jesus spoke it, and came forth, still bound by the grave clothes (John 11:33–44).

I cannot help but imagine how this miracle was received. People would have been stunned.

"How could it be?"

"No one has ever returned from the grave, not after four days in the tomb!"

"I can hardly believe it, and I wouldn't believe it if I hadn't seen it with my own eyes."

What of Martha and Mary? Surely they would have felt unspeakable joy. But eventually they would have had to resume normal life again. The text says nothing about what followed. But we know from personal experience that no family is perfect. Lazarus returned to his sisters as he was, and they welcomed him back as they were, which means that Lazarus irritated them once again, that Martha continued to fuss, and Mary kept neglecting household responsibilities. As it turns out, the miracle was a temporary solution; not only did Lazarus die again, but the characters in the story resumed their roles and returned to the habits they had before the ordeal began.

Reversal

Martha and Mary wanted a miracle, which they understood as a reversal of the normal course of events—in their case, Lazarus's sickness and eventual death. We imagine miracles in exactly that way, as a reversal of something we don't want, which then gives way to something we do want. Such is the nature of our longings after a loss; in most cases we want to reclaim life as it once was. But we discover soon enough that even resuscitation, however spectacular, would fail to deliver everything we want. Like winning the lottery, it would change the circumstances but not necessarily the recipients—not you, not your family, not your friends. If you were irritable before the miracle occurred, you would be irritable afterwards, and probably sooner rather than later; if angry, you would eventually show flashes of anger again; if self-pitying, you would find something to complain about. A miraculous reversal of fortune can only accomplish so much. Eventually life returns to normal, human nature to its old ways.

Miracles manifest God's power and alter circumstances, often dramatically; but the absence of miracles can do good work as well—just work of a different kind. I wonder what might have happened if Jesus had waited two years rather than a mere four days before resuscitating Lazarus. By then life would have been very different, very much changed. I can only imagine how a conversation between Lazarus and Martha might have unfolded.

"You've changed, Martha. You seem calmer and quieter. What has happened to you?"

"I fussed a lot after you died, until it became simply intolerable, to me and to everyone else. I worried and worked all the time until I became too exhausted to do any more. Then God spoke to me."

"What did he say?"

"He told me to listen."

"Listen?"

"Yes, listen. To him. I had to learn to be quiet. I started to meditate on the Psalms. My heart stopped racing. I learned how to rest. Oh Lazarus, I missed you so much. But I realized I missed your sickness, too. I almost needed you to be sick so that I could take care of you. When you died I not only lost you, I lost myself, too. I lost my reason for living. It took me a long time to find another reason. It was so hard, but so wonderful, too."

"Do you really want me to stay, Martha?"

"Of course I do, Lazarus. I have never stopped missing you. But your death forced me to face myself. It forced me to change. I want that, too."

I wonder how many times in human history someone, looking back over the years on some tragedy, has spoken similarly. "I want my old life back again ... But I want the change that occurred because I suffered the tragedy, too." How strange that is.

Rarely in the biblical story do we observe miracles having a uniformly good effect, not because the miracles themselves are somehow flawed, but because miracles can and often do expose a major weakness in human nature — the desire to control God. Miracles can give the impression that God is ready and willing to perform for us on cue, to satisfy our every wish and whim, and to meet our demands as if he were a personal genie. We need look no further than the pages of Scripture for examples of this dynamic.

The ancient Hebrews witnessed miracle after miracle — the ten plagues, the parting of the Red Sea, manna from Heaven, water from a rock, conquest of enemies — to the point that they assumed miracles were theirs by right. But that spirit of entitlement led to nothing but disbelief and complaint whenever they faced a new hardship. Likewise, Jesus' followers were rarely satisfied when he performed miracles because they always seemed to want more. Enough was never enough. When Jesus was arrested, tried, and crucified, the very people who had witnessed his miracles turned on him. His miracles didn't make them faithful followers, not even in the case of his closest friends.

My kids called or wrote in response to the email I sent commemorating Diana Jane's birthday. They thanked me, as they always do on such occasions. Like me, they wonder what life would be like if Diana Jane were still alive. Catherine would have a sister; John would have someone closer to him in age. Her presence would affect the entire dynamic of the home, no doubt for the good. Then again, her absence has done that too. It could have turned out tragically, and I could be writing words of lament right now instead of words of gratitude. But it did not turn out tragically, not in the long run anyway, though the event itself was, and still is, tragic. We feel sorrow, to be sure; but it is a sweet sorrow. We are aware of the loss but grateful for the outcome. It is a tension we have learned to embrace.

This is the great irony of tragedy and miracle. Tragedy can actually have a good effect, and miracle a negative one. I have often told my children that if their mother were to return today, she would be so proud. She would see who they have become, and she would celebrate them. I think she would also laugh, especially at me. I remember our many arguments about division of labor in the home. I was clueless about what it takes to manage a home, deferring—selfishly, I must admit—to her. I assumed she was manager and I was her assistant, which she rejected as sexist and unfair.

Today, she would find ample evidence to support her contention that women are no more genetically predisposed and naturally gifted to fold laundry, cook meals, or clean the house than men. "See," she would say, "you did it! I was right all along." Tragedy tore her from us, but it also worked good into us. No doubt God would have accomplished his will if she had lived, only another way. Which is exactly the point: what matters is his will, not our vision of ideal circumstances that we claim as a right and then demand of God.

Lazarus was restored to life, a miracle if ever there was one. But he eventually died again. His resuscitation was not the real miracle of the story. In his conversation with Martha, Jesus claimed that he was the resurrection and the life—a miracle of a higher order, for in the resurrection death was not postponed for a season but conquered. No one had to roll the stone away from Jesus' tomb; no one had to remove the grave clothes; no one had to mourn his death again after months or years of life. The resurrection was not a reversal but a transformation, the firstfruits of a great harvest, the portal through which we see into eternity and a bridge to a greater world.

The apostle John referred to Jesus' miracles as "signs." Signs point beyond themselves to something else. The feeding of the five thousand was a sign, for the people who ate bread that day became hungry again. The healing of the blind man was a sign, for the man who received his sight eventually lost it again — if not before, then certainly at death. It is Jesus who is true bread, Jesus who is true light, Jesus who is true life. The true miracle of every story is Jesus. He is more than a sign; he is God's kingdom come to earth, demonstrating that it is real and true and powerful.

Heaven is the end for which we long, and Jesus is the bridge to it. He came from Heaven to earth, from three dimensions to two, and then returned to Heaven, two dimensions being absorbed into three. In Jesus we see sign pointing to reality, resuscitation giving way to resurrection, shadow being swallowed up by glorious light. But Jesus is more than the bridge who gets us across. He is the destination too. In seeing him as he is, we will become like him.

Resurrection Life

The longing for a miracle, then, is really a longing for Heaven; we want more than a resuscitation that will restore a loved one to us, more than bread that will satisfy our appetite for a few hours, more than water that will quench our thirst on a sultry afternoon. We want more than a temporary reversal, which only puts off the inevitable for a short time. Our longings run deeper than we think; our deepest desire is not for mere signs but for what the signs point to. We want Heaven, which Jesus' resurrection guarantees.

Jesus came once to die for sin, conquer death, and win our salvation. He will come again to establish the kingdom in all its perfection. This final kingdom will not be lesser than this life, a kind of phantom state of existence; it will be more, having a quality that far surpasses what goes by the name of "life" as we know it now. As Paul argued, everything in the universe has a body that is appropriate for its time, place, and role. He writes:

> Not all flesh is the same. People have one kind of flesh, animals have another, birds another and fish another. There are also heavenly bodies and there are earthly bodies; but the splendor of the heavenly bodies is one kind, and the splendor of the earthly bodies is another. The sun has one kind of splendor, the moon another and the stars another; and star differs from star in splendor. (1 Corinthians 15:39–41)

The resurrection will usher in a new kind of embodiment, one that is perfect, complete, and eternal, fit for the new age of the kingdom. What was two dimensional will become three dimensional; what was flat and fragile, subject to decay and death, will become robust, powerful, and permanent. Paul writes, "The body that is sown is perishable, it is raised imperishable; it is sown in dishonor, it is raised in glory; it is sown in weakness, it is raised in power; it is sown a natural body, it is raised a spiritual body" (1 Corinthians 15:42–44). In this case "spiritual body" does not refer to something insubstantial and shadowy, almost ghostlike, but to something solid and real, something fit for life in Heaven. In *The Great Divorce*, C. S. Lewis argues that Heaven is so real newcomers will find it uncomfortably solid and heavy, real beyond anything they had ever known and experienced on earth, just as a person finds sunshine blinding after spending an afternoon in a dark movie theater.

Heaven: Accept No Substitutes

This all seems hopeful and encouraging, and so it is. But I am not finished yet. Here I want to offer a gentle word of warning, as much to me as to you. Though we do long for Heaven, we must resist confusing sign and reality, resuscitation and resurrection, shadow and substance. In short, we must hold out for the *real* Heaven—Heaven not just for our benefit but for the world's benefit; Heaven not simply for now but for all eternity. When our longing for Heaven drives us to seek out lesser substitutes, we are headed for trouble. There are two especially menacing dangers we need to be aware of: reducing Heaven to a personal kingdom and seeking to establish an earthly utopia.

Danger 1: Reducing Heaven to a Personal Kingdom

Our longing for Heaven can become a danger when we reduce it to a personal kingdom for me, mine, or ours, which will cause us to settle for and find satisfaction in a limited redemptive story — one that fulfills our interests and longings but not necessarily the interests and longings of the rest of the world. We land the perfect job, but then forget about the people who don't have jobs and maybe can't find jobs. We marry and have children, but then forget about the people who long for the same. We win awards and make lots of money and move into an upscale neighborhood, but then forget about the hundreds of millions of people who live on a few dollars a day. Once the redemptive story turns out well for us, we tend to forget about the other people God loves. It is so easy to forget. I am tempted to call it selfishness, but that strikes me as too harsh. It is more the case that we suffer from myopia; we fail to see much beyond ourselves.

Over the past month, Patricia and I have welcomed every one of our five kids home for at least one visit. We have enjoyed long conversations over meals and invited friends to join us for barbecues. Much has changed over the past year or two. My daughter Catherine is married and pregnant; David recently married, and John is about to. Catherine is teaching junior high, David and John are working at nonprofits. Patricia's daughter Morgan teaches at a Spanish language immersion school, and her daughter Taylor—the youngest of our collective five—is about to graduate from university. They enjoy rich friendships, belong to good churches, and have a sturdy faith. All seems well.

But is doing well really the point of redemption? Can we reduce redemption exclusively to an individual and personal experience? I still think about the years when life seemed far more difficult, a redemptive outcome far less certain. What about people whose stories seem to consist of little more than one loss and problem after another? Not that I should feel guilt or shame over the relative stability and prosperity my family enjoys. I embrace it as a gift from God. But it is *a sign* of redemption, not the thing itself in all its finality and perfection. It points beyond itself to something else, something greater. That something greater is Heaven, the true end of the redemptive story, the object of our deepest longings.

In the meantime, God calls us to be servants and stewards. The Reformed tradition uses the term "common grace" to describe the gifts God so generously gives to all people, regardless of their worthiness. Jesus said that God himself "causes his sun to rise on the evil and the good, and sends rain on the righteous and the unrighteous" (Matthew 5:45). But God does not distribute these gifts evenly and equally, as is so palpably and painfully evident, for some receive far more than others.

Perhaps God distributes his gifts unequally to provide us

with the opportunity to close the gap between the "much" that we have and the "little" that others have. Paul seems to make exactly that point. The Corinthian church had promised to contribute to the needs of the poverty-stricken community in Jerusalem, but they had not delivered on their promise. Here is Paul's word to them: "For if the willingness is there, the gift is acceptable according to what one has, not according to what one does not have. Our desire is not that others might be relieved while you are hard pressed, but that there might be equality. At the present time your plenty will supply what they need, so that in turn their plenty will supply what you need" (2 Corinthians 8:12–14).

One of my favorite church fathers is John Chrysostom (347–407), the godly, passionate, and moralistic patriarch of Constantinople. Known as the greatest preacher in antiquity, he served as patriarch for only a few years before the imperial family sent him into exile, largely because he called them to account for their indulgent and luxurious living. He did not condemn wealth as such, but he did challenge the wealthy to be faithful stewards. Bounty, he said, implies responsibility:

> Faith tells us that God alone can supply the material things on which we depend. He gives some people more than they need, not that they can enjoy great luxury, but to make them stewards of his bounty on behalf of orphans, the sick, and the crippled. If they are bad stewards, keeping this bounty to themselves, they will become poor in spirit, and their hearts will fill with

misery. If they are good stewards, they will become rich in spirit, their hearts filling with joy.[17]

Prosperity and success for me and mine is not Heaven, only a sign of Heaven. It will turn into hell if I fail to use my bounty to serve others.

Danger 2: Seeking to Establish an Earthly Utopia

Our longings for Heaven can also become a danger when we strive to establish Heaven on earth prematurely, in effect substituting a human institution — the state, for example — for God's righteousness and merciful rule. A human creation takes the place of God's kingdom, with disastrous consequences. The past two centuries have produced hundreds of such utopian experiments, some catastrophically evil. Nazi Germany, Stalinist Russia, and Maoist China come to mind as three terrifying examples.

The problem is almost too obvious to state. Utopias promise a heaven for some but not for all — for the powerful at the expense of the powerless, for the rich at the expense of the poor, for the healthy at the expense of the weak. Perhaps using the examples of Nazi Germany, Stalinist Russia, and Maoist China might seem extreme to you. Admittedly, they are extreme, though it is sobering to consider the power and influence these regimes once had. Still, I'm not sure respectable people like you and me are any less susceptible to this danger; our utopias are simply less cruel, less destructive, and less obvious. Anything that replaces God is not Heaven but an idol. It is easy to identify these utopias, too, for they always exalt themselves at the expense of what the Bible refers to as "the least of these."

Heaven will not arrive in all its glory until Jesus himself returns. In the meantime, what should we do? Somehow we must learn to live for God and his kingdom in a world that is far from heavenly. On occasion we will pass through periods of relative peace; all will appear well, though we should not allow ourselves to be lured by such peace into complacency and selfishness. God gives us those peaceful stretches of time —my family happens to be in one right now—so we can devote our resources and energies, unimpeded by serious difficulty and opposition, to advancing his kingdom. But the peace will not last forever. Sooner or later we will plunge headlong into a world that is not at all peaceful.

A Resistance Movement

How should we then live, considering the in-between time in which we find ourselves, suspended, as we are, between Christ's first coming and his second coming? Before considering this question directly, I invite you to picture yourself in an imaginary scene from the days of World War II.

You live in a French town. It is a warm June day. You are strolling toward the market, located in the central town square, to buy lunch. It is Monday, and the market is teeming with a crowd that seems strangely quiet and subdued. Your eyes glance furtively from side to side. You notice small groups of German soldiers whispering to each other, all the while scanning the crowd suspiciously. You have never seen them looking this nervous and angry. You see fear in their faces. Large banners displaying the swastika hang on many buildings, and a loud speaker alternates between playing music and blaring propaganda about German superiority and Nazi victories. You wander through the market, stopping to chat with a few friends and merchants, and finally buy a scrap of cheese, a baguette, and a bottle of wine, looking around as casually as you can. Out of the corner of your eye you see someone staring at you. Immediately he looks away, scratches his head, and then nods in a particular direction before wandering off.

You linger for a while, and then you too wander off, making your way to the other side of the market. You walk down a street and several alleys, finally sitting down at a park bench to eat the cheese and the baguette. Waiting perhaps fifteen minutes, you look around the corner to see if anyone has followed you. Convinced you are alone, you walk to a door and knock three times, then three times again, and finally twice. A man opens the door and lets you in, quickly and quietly closing the door behind you. He leads you up three flights of stairs and into the kitchen of an apartment. You smell coffee and cigarettes, and you notice that the drapes are drawn, the windows closed. You hear a fly buzzing, caught between a drape and a window. Seven people —four men, three women—sit around the table, sipping coffee. They are in the middle of a conversation.

"The Nazis are nervous," one says. "Everyone feels the tension."

"They have reason to be nervous," you chime in.

They all turn their heads towards you. "Then it's true," someone says.

"Yes, true. My information is absolutely reliable. The allies landed at Normandy a few days ago and have secured a beachhead. They won't be turned back; the tide has turned. It is only a matter of time before the Nazis are defeated. Churchill will settle for nothing less than total victory."

"Shall we listen to Radio Free Europe? It will provide a detailed report we can trust, unlike the propaganda we hear every day around here."

"Not now. Too risky. Let's go over our assignments."

"We need to get word out, quietly of course, to those loyal to the cause, and try to recruit more people. It will be easier now that the allies have landed in Europe. We need to continue the work of sabotage—you know, pollute petrol, ruin or steal supplies, slash tires, disrupt communication. Anything to distract and frustrate and undermine."

"And keep smuggling Jews out of France and into Portugal?"

"Exactly. They are in more danger now than ever. In fact, all of us face greater danger now. A wounded animal always fights more viciously. We can't allow ourselves to be intimidated or discouraged."

"Viva la France!" you whisper. The rest nod their heads. "Liberation is near, freedom around the corner. Let's fight on."

The scene is imaginary but accurately reflects the facts of what happened and the vital role of the French Resistance in defeating Hitler and ending the war. I wanted you to experience a small taste of what it might have been like because as Christians I believe we would do well to consider ourselves as members of a similar kind of resistance movement.

For now, we reside in one kingdom, but we belong to another. We refuse to yield to the ruler of this world — a pretender and usurper — even though he boasts that he will remain in power for a thousand years. We know there is another kingdom because our king came to this world, defeated the enemies of sin and death, and then returned to his heavenly kingdom to continue his work on our behalf. Evil remains but it has already lost the war. The true king has appeared, the victory is coming, and the end is in sight. Our calling is to participate in a resistance movement, support the final liberation of enemy-occupied territory, and help establish God's kingdom.

One of my favorite early Christian documents dates to the middle of the second century. Entitled the *The So-Called Letter to Diognetus*, it describes how early Christians served, influenced, and thrived in a hostile culture. It captures very well what it means to belong to a resistance movement, what it means to live in an earthly country and culture but still belong to the kingdom:

> For Christians cannot be distinguished from the rest of the human race by country or language or custom. They

do not live in cities of their own; they do not use a peculiar form of speech; they do not follow an eccentric manner of life ... They live in their own countries, but only as aliens. They have a share in everything as citizens, and endure everything as foreigners. Every foreign land is their fatherland, and yet for them every fatherland is a foreign land.[18]

We do this when we welcome the least of these into our homes, when we devote our time, talent, and money to kingdom causes, and when we invest our energy into obeying the Great Commandment and fulfilling the Great Commission, thus laying up for ourselves "treasures in heaven."

Establishing the Kingdom of Heaven

As members of God's resistance movement, we are not alone. We have the presence of Jesus and the power of the Holy Spirit to help and encourage us along the way. We have a record of God's redemptive story. We have the sacraments — water, bread, wine, and oil — that serve as sign, seal, and conduit of God's grace. And we have the church, the community of faith, which belongs to Jesus, bears witness to his saving work, provides us with good companions, and builds outposts for his kingdom.

We have work to do, too. Jesus commands us to proclaim him as Lord and invest our lives in a Heaven that still seems a long ways off, a Heaven that Jesus—and only Jesus—can establish.

> The kingdom of heaven is like treasure hidden in a field. When a man found it, he hid it again, and then in his joy went and sold all he had and bought that field.
>
> Again, the kingdom of heaven is like a merchant looking for fine pearls. When he found one of great value, he went away and sold everything he had and bought it. (Matthew 13:44–46)

Establishing the kingdom will not be easy. God's kingdom often seems remote, weak, insignificant, tiny as a mustard seed. Jesus tells us, however, that it will not always be so. "The kingdom of heaven is like a mustard seed, which a man took and planted in his field. Though it is the smallest of all seeds, yet when it grows, it is the largest of garden plants and becomes a tree, so that the birds come and perch in its branches" (Matthew 13:31–32).

This tension between what seems insignificant now and what promises one day to be overwhelmingly significant forces me to ask, almost daily, *What is real? What is right? What is true?* I know what I am sometimes tempted to think: the real is what exists immediately before me. The real is the suffering I face, or the real is the success and prosperity I enjoy. But is it? No, the real is God's rule, his coming kingdom, Heaven itself. If it is real, we should live for it every day and conform ourselves to it as members of a resistance movement, who eagerly await the return of the king and his rightful rule.

What we do for the kingdom makes a difference, even though it might not seem to. Paul assures us that our work for the kingdom matters, not only for this life but also for eternity. It will have a kind of "carry over" effect in the age to come. Nothing we do will be in vain if done for the kingdom. He writes, "Therefore, my dear brothers and sisters, stand firm. Let nothing move you. Always give yourselves fully to the work of the Lord, because you know that your labor in the Lord is not in vain" (1 Corinthians 15:58). Our labor will not be in vain because God himself will include and envelop it in his ultimate plan to establish his kingdom, absorbing our efforts, as feeble as they are, into something great and glorious.

When my kids were little, they liked to assist me in the various projects I had to do around the house. Their favorite was painting. They would slop paint and make designs on the walls with great enthusiasm, dripping a good bit of it on the drop cloth in the process and putting paint in places where paint didn't belong. Eventually they would lose interest and wander off to do something else. Then I would scramble to repair the damage and complete the job. When they returned later they would say, "Look at what we did, Dad! We did such a good job. It looks beautiful." They were right to say it too, for they did in fact help. My work didn't nullify theirs; I only absorbed it into mine.

God sees and treats our work in the same way. What we do for God and his kingdom is not a waste, not trivial, token, or meaningless. Our work as parents, neighbors, students, teachers, contractors, business executives, laborers, lawyers, doctors, and volunteers really does count, or at least can if done for the kingdom. It is not insignificant; it is merely inadequate, imperfect, and incomplete. Heaven will not nullify our labor; it will take it up into something grander and greater, two dimensions becoming three.

The book of Revelation tells a story of conflict, but its vision of the end is glorious:

> Then I saw "a new heaven and a new earth," for the first heaven and the first earth had passed away, and there was no longer any sea. I saw the Holy City, the new Jerusalem, coming down out of heaven from God, prepared as a bride beautifully dressed for her husband. And I heard a loud voice from the throne saying, "Look! God's dwelling place is now among the people, and he will dwell with them. They will be his people, and God himself will be with them and be their God. 'He will wipe every tear from their eyes. There will be no more death' or mourning or crying or pain, for the old order of things has passed away." (Revelation 21:1–4)

It is the vision of Heaven, the kingdom come to earth, making all things well and whole, for all peoples.

A few years ago I digitized several thousand old photos, including hundreds taken of our summer trips. I recently came across a photo of that magical and evocative place we discovered while driving down the California coast. It bears witness to the fact that the photo that hung on the pantry door did in fact point to a real place — real as no photo could ever hope to be—for we saw and experienced it for ourselves. Heaven, our true home and final destiny, will be real in the same way, only more so, so real that it will make us hurt with joy. It will swallow up everything that is good in earthly existence, making it gloriously and permanently pure, perfect, and complete.

CHAPTER 11

The Middle of the Story

I wish I could end this book as neatly and tidily as a children's story, assuring you that from this moment on you will live "happily ever after." But as you well know, I can't. And you wouldn't believe me if I did. Eventually, we will live happily ever after, but only when the redemptive story ends, which seems a long way off. In the meantime, you and I are somewhere in the middle of the story, as if stuck in the chaos and messiness of a half-finished home improvement project. We might have one chapter left in our story, or we might have fifty. We could experience more of the same for years to come, or we could be on the verge of a change so dramatic that if we knew about it we would faint with fear or wonder, or perhaps both. We could be entering the happiest phase of our lives, or the saddest. We simply don't know and can't know. I'm not even sure we would want to know.

What does it mean for us to be somewhere in the middle of the story? How should we respond, knowing we won't be able to avoid stretches of time in which life will seem as confusing as a puzzle missing half its pieces? In my mind, there is only one good option: *we must choose to stay in the redemptive story*. However unclear it might be to us, we can trust that God is writing the story — a story so grand, glorious, and beautiful that only faith will enable us to believe it and stay in it. We might not be able to see a redemptive thread running through it, which will tempt us to take control of the story ourselves. Still, it is in such moments that we must choose to read our story in light of *the* story, to believe that God is good, powerful, and wise, even when he appears to be mean or absent, and to keep hope alive that all will be well.

Because all in fact will be well. Isn't that how the biblical story reads and what the resurrection promises?

An example comes to my mind that shows us something of what it means to be in the middle of the story. It is another story about a visit to a prison, except in this case the story does not end as cleanly as Sunday's story (chapter 2). It is more like the story you and I are living out, full of peril and promise, ambiguity and hope. The story is Tricia's; she gave me permission to tell it to you. It is admittedly dramatic; yet Tricia had to learn to live out the story in the ordinariness of life, trusting that God would work redemption.

Tricia attended the same college as her sister, Susie, in the late 1980s. They lived across the street from each other in campus housing and spent a great deal of time together. Susie was not one to skip class, so when she failed to show up for the first class of a new semester, Tricia decided to check in on her. Finding the door of her room ajar, she entered and discovered a grisly scene. Susie was dead, the victim of a brutal rape and murder. Tricia later discovered that the assailant was a man named Jeff, someone Susie had met while working in a drug rehabilitation program. He had an extensive history of alcohol and drug abuse as well as of sexual violence. Jeff was arrested, tried, convicted, and sentenced to prison for Susie's rape and murder.

The trauma catapulted Tricia into a crisis of faith. As a new Christian, she could not reconcile the good God she knew with the evil rape and murder of her sister. She swung wildly between denial and despair. "Over the years," she wrote to me, "I found myself either remembering Susie with joy while hanging onto denial, or sinking into dark despair about her death while denying her life, faith, or anything hopeful." Somehow she managed to press on; she graduated from college, married, and had children. But some ten years later something snapped inside her, pushing her into a terrible darkness. She was forced to face the loss once again, as if in "vivid color and emotion." She literally "came to the end of herself," which drove her into the arms of God. "Once denial was gone and the reality of my broken heart obvious, God became very real and personal—the truth and teachings of Jesus my lifeline."

Still, the memory of Susie's murder and murderer hovered in the back of her mind and continued to menace her. She realized that she had to do something to face the fear, address the bitterness, and find freedom from the spirit of revenge that permeated her life. She heard of a program that would allow her to confront the perpetrator under the supervision of a team of experts. She signed up for the program because she wanted peace.

The meeting between Jeff and Tricia lasted six hours.

Jeff went first. He told parts of his life story, which Tricia described as excruciatingly sad, and then related the events of the fateful day. Tricia asked questions—why he targeted her sister, what he did, and how he did it. She drilled him for details to mollify an imagination that had taunted and tormented her for years. She knew she had to learn what happened to her sister and stare it down, and she wanted to stand with Susie in her suffering and to grieve with her, as if witnessing the horrible event firsthand.

After breaking for lunch, it was Tricia's turn. She talked for two hours, describing the close relationship she had with Susie, the faith they shared together, the trauma she had experienced in finding Susie's body, the rage and fear she felt. She talked about the deep struggle of faith she had to endure. She showed photos and told stories, evoking so much emotion that Jeff actually began to cry.

After five hours of intense conversation, Tricia and Jeff fell silent, having nothing more to say. They were exhausted, wrung out like rags squeezed dry. The conversation was done, the business finished, at least for them. But not for God. "The final hour of the meeting belonged to God alone," Tricia told me. She had satisfied her desire to learn the details; she had confronted her sister's murderer; she had put her acute suffering to rest. It seemed a chapter in her redemptive story was coming to an end.

Only then did she realize that Jeff also had a story, and his could be as redemptive as hers. His suffering, too, could be put to rest. Tricia discovered in that moment that God wanted her to tell Jeff what she believed—for his sake, not for hers. So she told Jeff about her faith, about the cross and the resurrection, about God's grace and mercy, which, as she put it, "could cover the whole mess." She told him that she had finally found liberation through forgiveness, Christ's forgiveness of her and her forgiveness of Jeff; he, too, could experience that same forgiveness if he wished. Christ had suffered punishment for her sins and his sins; Christ had the power to turn a story of violence and evil into a story of redemption. God could overcome darkness with light, wrongdoing with forgiveness, suffering with healing. He had for her; he could for him, too. "The glory of God's love overcame my worst fear." In the end Jeff could only say, "I know this doesn't make any of this pain go away, but I need to say it. I am sorry. I am so ... so sorry."

Then Tricia left. She has not seen or spoken to Jeff since, sensing that he is "on his own path now, released to God." Who knows what will happen to Jeff in the years to come? Will he become a Christian or dismiss the Christian faith as so much nonsense? Will he become "the man God designed him to be" or slip ever deeper into selfishness and ugliness? Will he commit himself to living a redemptive life or continue on the same course? Who knows what will happen to Tricia, too? Will she descend into darkness yet again? Will she discover that she must forgive Jeff one more time, or many more times? Might Tricia's future vocation emerge out of the experience? How will her story unfold in the years to come, even if she does believe that God has "the last word"?

Will Tricia and Jeff have to meet yet again, which seems likely, this time if (or when) the Department of Human Services decides to hold a hearing before a judge, pushing for Jeff's release.

Tricia's story seems messy and incomplete, which is true of all our stories, living, as we are, in the middle of them. There is so much we don't know, so much we can't see. It is this uncertainty that might tempt us to step out of the redemptive story and pursue another one. We have other options at our disposal, as we well know; we have other stories we could follow. You probably know what they are, too. We could choose a story of despair, resigning ourselves to a life of disappointment, defeat, and misery because life has not turned out as we wanted and expected. Or we could choose a story of compromise, settling for a "nice" life rather than a redemptive one, nice because it has turned out reasonably well for us, though not necessarily well for the rest of the world. Or we could choose a story of control, insisting on our way rather than submitting to God's way, even though we might make lots of people unhappy along the way.

In short, we could choose to step out of the redemptive story, not allowing enough time to see it unfold to the end. It is, after all, hard to stay in the story, considering the cost involved.

Such is the temptation Joseph faced. The biblical story of Joseph has always been one of my favorites. His final words, spoken to his brothers, have never stopped echoing in my mind: "You intended to harm me, but God intended it for good to accomplish what is now being done, the saving of many lives" (Genesis 50:20). If there has ever been a redemptive story, Joseph's is one that follows the script almost perfectly.

Still, it is easy to forget that it actually happened to Joseph, unfolding over a long period of time. We can read it in half an hour, but Joseph *lived* it, and he had no idea how it would turn out. I try to get inside his experience as best I can. What was it like for him to be betrayed by his brothers? To be sold as a slave? To be imprisoned for honoring his master and guarding the purity of his master's wife? I ponder his suffering, which lasted for years—far longer than I can imagine and would have been able to endure. This is no sweet and sentimental story, not if you get inside it.

I am especially curious about one incident in the course of the narrative, so insignificant that it hardly seems worthy of notice. But Joseph certainly noticed it. It was just the sort of experience that could break a person. As the story goes, two men from Pharaoh's court, the cupbearer and the baker, were imprisoned for some impropriety. Both had dreams, so confusing that they had no idea how to interpret them. Joseph noticed how troubled they were and inquired about their distress. Telling Joseph their dreams, they were surprised to discover that God had given Joseph the ability to interpret them. Joseph predicted a favorable outcome in the case of the cupbearer's dream, an unfavorable one in the case of the baker's dream.

Then Joseph implored the cupbearer to remember him

before Pharaoh when he was restored to his position of authority, which the cupbearer promised to do. It was a reasonable request, to be sure, considering the service Joseph rendered to the cupbearer and the years he spent suffering in prison for crimes he had never committed. But the cupbearer forgot his promise, and Joseph remained in prison.

It must have been profoundly disappointing and disillusioning to Joseph, who could have given up on God there and then. God dangled freedom in front of Joseph's face, awakening hope and longing, and then yanked it away, as if he were an abusive parent. Joseph had remained faithful to God, but God had not returned the favor. Why trust God any more? What would be gained by it?

Joseph knew nothing of the future, of course. How could he? He knew nothing of Egypt's years of bounty and famine, of Pharaoh's disturbing dream, of Joseph's promotion to a high position in the court, of his supervision over the collection and distribution of grain, of reconciliation with his brothers and reunion with his father. At that point he knew only his immediate experience — the cupbearer's forgetfulness and selfishness, more years in prison with no end in sight, suffering and darkness. Joseph had to make a choice: trust God or abandon faith? Believe God's story or follow another one? Joseph chose to stay in the story, though his chance for deliverance appeared to have come and gone.

If Joseph had been released when he had hoped and expected to be, the story would have turned out well for him, to be sure, but only for him. In all likelihood, Joseph would have never seen his brothers and father again, never assumed a high position of responsibility in the court, never rescued an entire nation from starvation. Such would have been the result—the price, really—of a premature ending to the story.

Like Joseph—and like you—I find myself in the middle of the story, just as I was twenty years ago when I teetered unknowingly on the precipice of catastrophe. Just today I told my son John in a telephone conversation that the story of the Sittser family is changing dramatically. Years ago I committed myself—my children would say "fiercely" so—to living out a redemptive story that involved four people rather than six. It turned out to be a pretty good story, too—so good, in fact, that I have resisted seeing it change.

It is too late for that now, for change is coming, whether or not I want it or like it. A long and arduous chapter has come to an end; a new one has begun. I married Patricia over a year ago. Catherine and David are also married, as I wrote in the last chapter, and John was married just a month ago. David gave his mother's engagement ring to Kelli, and John is wearing a wedding band that has been in the family for generations, worn by his great uncle John and his great-grandfather Charles. Patricia's girls are thriving as well. Morgan and Taylor have regular dinners together with my son John and his wife, Annalise; they identify themselves as the "Seattle Chapter" of the family.

A few weeks ago Catherine gave birth to Gideon, the first member of the next generation of the family. Patricia and I left the day of the delivery to visit Catherine and Jacob in Portland and to welcome Gideon into the fold. Words fail to express what it was like to see my daughter as a mother and to hold Gideon for the first time. I was so proud of her, so immediately fond of him.

The next morning Patricia and Jacob left the hospital room to have breakfast together, leaving me alone with Catherine and Gideon. I held the baby while Catherine dozed. Sunlight peeked through the closed blinds, filling the room with soft light. All was quiet and peaceful; silence filled the room as if it were air. I felt almost weightless, floating in a cavernous cathedral, breathing pure oxygen.

Then I remembered. The sweet silence of that hospital room reminded me of that *other*, heavy silence of twenty years ago, full of terror and sadness, the silence of the emergency vehicle that transported us from the scene of the accident to the hospital.

Suddenly I was suspended between two worlds — two moments in time, two weighty events, two experiences of silence, separated by twenty years. In one I was looking forward, staring into an abyss of confusion and darkness; in the other I was looking backward, tracing a narrative, now bathed in light, that had led up to the deliciously beautiful scene I was then enjoying. I kept seeing snapshots of Catherine — as a baby with her mother, as a bewildered little girl having lost her mother, as a confused teenager and curious college student, as Maria in *The Sound of Music* and a pianist playing at various competitions, as a teacher in a chaotic classroom in Bogota, as a bride on her wedding day, as a new mother asleep before my very eyes. Not surprisingly, the same texts began to echo in my mind as they had before, reminding me that my story does not stand on its own, nor ever did; it is and always has been firmly rooted in another story, a bigger and better story, *the* story. My story only stands as a witness to the redemptive story.

I looked at Gideon, who stirred and whimpered softly. Catherine turned in her bed, opened her eyes, and smiled at me before drifting off once again to sleep. The silence returned, whispering this verse from the Psalms:

> Truly my soul finds rest in God;
>   my salvation comes from him.
> Truly he is my rock and my salvation;
>   he is my fortress, I will never be shaken.
>   (Psalm 62:1–2)

I have no idea how the story will unfold in the years to come. I am as blind now as I was twenty years ago. I can be certain only of this: though the story will not turn out as I expect and plan, it will be redemptive all the same. We might be in the middle of that story, uncertain of what looms ahead; but God rules over the whole thing, which is all that matters. For God is the author of the redemptive story; we know who this God is, too, because he entered the story as a character and turned the plot in a startlingly new direction. Jesus Christ came to redeem the world—to reclaim, renew, and restore it until all is complete, whole, and perfect. Such is the plot of the redemptive story as told in the Bible.

It is a strange story, too, because, though still unfolding, it is already finished. Christ has already accomplished what he wants to do in us; Christ has already transformed what he seeks to change in us day by day. Redemption means becoming who we already are in Christ. We are new, so we can become new; we are perfect, so we can become perfect. The weathered tree I described in the first chapter was once a small seed that contained everything it needed for what it would eventually become; it only grew into itself over time, shaped by the elements. Likewise, the figures Michelangelo wished to sculpt already existed in that stone; his work consisted of releasing them from the marble in which they were entombed. Once again, Paul's words come to mind, summarizing what is at the heart of redemption:

> So from now on we regard no one from a worldly point of view. Though we once regarded Christ in this way, we do so no longer. Therefore, if anyone is in Christ, the new creation has come: The old has gone, the new is here! (2 Corinthians 5:16–17)

Notes

1. John Cassian, in *The Conferences of John Cassian: The Wisdom of the Desert* (Bloomington, IN: Xlibris, 2000), 170–71.

2. Ibid., 174.

3. John Calvin, *Institutes of the Christian Religion* (ed. John T. McNeill; trans. Ford Lewis Battles; Philadelphia: Westminster, 1960), 722.

4. Ibid., 700.

5. Thomas Merton, *New Seeds of Contemplation* (New York: New Directions, 1962), 258.

6. Ibid.

7. Athanasius, *On the Incarnation* (Crestwood, NY: St. Vladimir's Seminary, 1993), 34.

8. Augustine, *The Confessions* (trans. Maria Boulding, O.S.B.; Hyde Park, NY: New City, 1997), 283.

9. C. S. Lewis, *The Great Divorce* (New York: Macmillan, 1946), 68.

10. Augustine, *The Confessions* (trans. Maria Boulding, O.S.B.; Hyde Park, NY: New City, 1997), 300.

11. John Steinbeck, *East of Eden* (New York: Penguin, 1952), 55.

12. Jean-Pierre de Caussade, *The Sacrament of the Present Moment* (San Francisco: Harper, 1966), 64.

13. Edward Yarnold, S.J., *The Awe-Inspiring Rites of Initiation: The Origins of the R.C.I.A.* (Collegeville, MN: Liturgical, 1994), 102.

14. Michael Counsell, ed., *2000 Years of Prayer* (Harrisburg, PA: Morehouse, 1999), 118.

15. Ibid., 179.

16. Ibid., 205.

17. Robert Van de Weyer, ed., *On Living Simply: The Golden Voice of John Chrysostom* (Liguori, MO: Liguori/Triumph, 1996), 6.

18. *The So-Called Letter to Diognetus*, in *Early Christian Fathers* (ed. Cyril C. Richardson; New York: Touchstone, 1996), 217.